“Addiction and urge
are possibilities rooted
in the thrownness
of Dasein.”

MARTIN HEIDEGGER

Being and Time

"It is enough to make
an honest soul vomit, as my
old friend the Garçon
used to say."

GUSTAVE FLAUBERT

Letters

"For then I go blind, blood veils my eyes and I hear what the great Gustave heard, the benches cracking in the court of the assizes."

SAMUEL BECKETT

Molloy

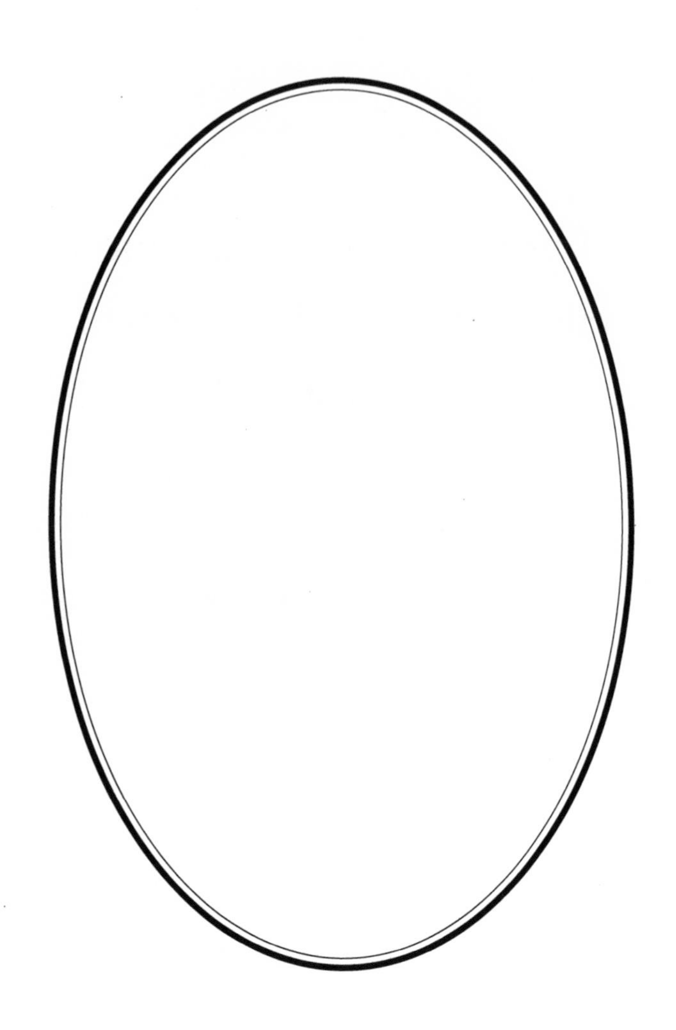

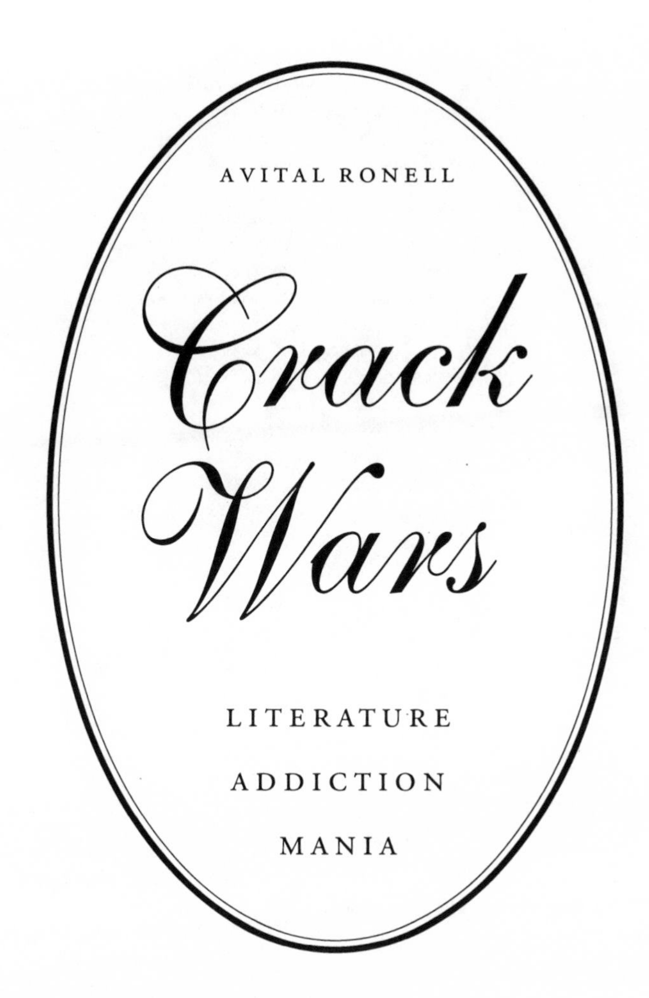

AVITAL RONELL

Crack Wars

LITERATURE
ADDICTION
MANIA

UNIVERSITY OF ILLINOIS PRESS

URBANA & CHICAGO

First Illinois paperback, 2004. Reprinted by arrangement with the Proprietor. Manufactured in the United States of America.
P 6 5 4 3 2 ♾ The book is printed on acid-free paper.

Library of Congress Cataloging in Publication Data
Ronell, Avital. Crack wars: literature, addiction, mania / Avital Ronell. p. cm. Originally published: Lincoln : University of Nebraska Press, 1992, in series: Texts and Contexts. Includes bibliographical references.
ISBN 10: 0-252-07190-5 (pbk. : alk. paper)/
ISBN 13: 978-0-252-07190-4 (pbk. : alk. paper).
1. Narcotics in literature. 2. Alcoholism in literature. 3. Drug abuse in literature. 4. Literature, Modern—History and Criticism. I. Title. PN56.N18 R66 2004
809'.933561—dc22 2003020605

CONTENTS

*or
The Transcendental Aesthetic
of the Thing to Be
Eaten

PART ONE : HITS

2 . 3

When he wanted to formulate the task of a philosophy yet to come, Friedrich Nietzsche committed this thought to writing: "Who will ever relate the whole history of narcotica?—It is almost the history of 'culture,' of our so-called high culture" (*The Gay Science,* § 86). Our work settles with this Nietzschean "almost"—the place where *narcotics* articulates a quiver between history and ontology.

Addiction will be our question: a certain type of "Being-on-drugs" that has everything to do with the bad conscience of our era.

4 · 5

Baudelaire assimilates intoxication to a concept of work.[1] Indeed, the plant puts you to work on a whole mnemonic apparatus. Intoxication names a method of mental labor that is responsible for making phantoms appear. It was a manner of treating the phantom, either by making it emerge—or vanish. It was by working on Edgar Allan Poe that Baudelaire recognized the logic of the tomb, to which he attached the stomach. The stomach *became* the tomb. At one point Baudelaire seems to ask: whom are you preserving in alcohol? This logic called for a resurrectionist memory, the supreme lucidity of intoxication, which arises when you have something in you that must be encrypted. Hence the ambivalent structure stimulant/tranquilizer.

6 . 7

When the body seems destined to experimentation, things are no longer introjected but trashed: dejected. The body proper regains its corruptible, organic status. Exposed to this mutability, the body cannot preserve its identity, but has a chance of seeing this fall, or ejection, sublimated or revalorized. Nautilus vs. the addict. When some bodies introduce drugs as a response to the call of addiction, every body is on the line: tampering and engineering, rebuilding and demolition, self-medication and vitamins become the occupations of every singularity. Sometimes the state has a hand in it.

8 . 9

We do not know how to renounce anything, Freud once observed. This type of relation to the object indicates an inability to mourn.

The addict is a non-renouncer par excellence (one thinks of the way *Goethe* mastered renunciation); yet, however haunted or hounded, the addict nonetheless establishes a partial separation from an invading presence.

IO.II

To gain access to the question of "Being-on-drugs" we have had to go the way of literature. We have chosen a work that exemplarily treats the persecutory object of an addiction. It does so within a fictional space, according to the fanatical exigency of realism. Few other works of fiction have brought out evidence of the pharmacodependency with which literature has always been secretly associated—as sedative, as cure, as escape conduit or euphorizing substance, as mimetic poisoning. There are many reasons for pressing literature on the narcotic question, but these are not essential: we could have just as easily followed the trajectory of *Rausch,* the ecstasy of intoxication, through the works of Kant, Nietzsche, and Heidegger on aesthetics. Or, guided by the philosophemes of forgetfulness, we could have traced the vertigo of the subject. Perhaps we would have arrived at the same results. Still, it is the case that the singular staging of the imaginary—"literature" in the widest sense—has a tradition of uncovering abiding structures of crime and ethicity with crucial integrity; one need only think of what Hegel drew from *Antigone* or Freud from *Oedipus Rex.* These works have always worked as informants but they were nobody's fools—they talked to the philosophers because they had inside knowledge. So literature, which is by no means an innocent bystander but often the accused, a breeding ground of hallucinogenres, has something to teach us about ethical fractures and the relationship to law. Gustave Flaubert's book went to court; it was denounced as a poison.[2]

12 . 13

On generalizing the notion of addiction. Our "drugs" uncover an implicit structure that was thought to be one technological extension among others, one legal struggle, or one form of cultural aberration. Classifiable in the plural (drugs: a singular plural), they were nonetheless expected to take place within a restricted economy.

What if "drugs" named a special mode of addiction, however, or the structure that is philosophically and metaphysically at the basis of our culture?

14 . 15

Crisis in immanence. Drugs, it turns out, are not so much about seeking an exterior, transcendental dimension—a fourth or fifth dimension—rather, they explore *fractal interiorities*. This was already hinted at by Burroughs's "algebra of need."

16 . 17

It has been said that the pervert does not do drugs.[3] Perhaps this refers to actions that are executed with guiltless precision.

18 . 19

Crack Wars. In an altogether uncanny manner, the polemics surrounding drugs historically became a War only when crack emerged. At this moment, drugs acquired the character of political question. Routinely associated with subversion, drugs, by means of crack, were escalated to the threat of revolution and a technological articulation of racial difference. Security was upped; civil liberties went down. Crack lost its specificity as merely one drug among others. As synecdoche of all drugs, crack illuminates an internal dimension of *polemos*—opening the apocalyptic horizon of the politics of drugs.

Prior to the emergence of what we call crack, drugs posed questions of control, legalization, and containment. Their usage seemed to belong to the socio-juridical precincts of *civil disobedience*. Ever since its inception as legal category, this all-American crime has earned its dose of moral defensibility from a link to anti-war activities. But crack, when it brought the War to drugs, brought war unto the law. Civil disobedience split away from constitutionally sanctioned habits: this war, unlike others, permits no dissent. Destructuring a civil constitution based on difference, crack introduces narcopolemics as total war.

20 . 21

A work, no matter how recondite, specialized, or antiquarian, manifests a historical compulsion. Of course, we no longer exist in a way that renders manifestation possible: we have lost access to what is manifested and even to manifestation itself. Nothing, today, can be manifested. Except, possibly, the fact that humanity is not yet just. The indecency of a humanism that goes on as if nothing had happened. The task of extremist writing is to put through the call for a justice of the future. Henceforth, Justice can no longer permit itself to be merely backward looking or bound in servility to sclerotic models and their modifications (their "future"). A justice of the future would have to show the will to rupture.

"A thinker," Flaubert said, "should have neither religion nor fatherland nor even any social conviction. Absolute scepticism."[4] Radically rupturing, the statement is not merely subversive. It does not depend upon the program which it criticizes. How might one free oneself from the cowardliness pressing upon social convictions of the present, subjugated as they are to reactive, mimetic, and regressive posturings?

22 . 23

On the noncontingency of addiction. Leaving aside the more obvious examples, we also have "proper" names: Proust (cortisone abuse); Walter Scott, Charles Dickens, Elizabeth Barrett Browning (frequent recourse to laudanum); Novalis, Kleist, Wackenroder ("soft" drugs); Voltaire and Balzac (coffee). Do these not point to the existence of a *toxic drive?* The need to ensure a temporality of addiction? The history of our culture as a problem in *narcossism*.

24 . 25

Crack disappoints the pleasure a drug might be expected to arouse. Hence the quality of crack as pure instance of "Being-on-drugs": it is only about producing a need for itself. If Freud was right about the apparent libidinal autonomy of the drug addict, then drugs are *libidinally invested.* To get off drugs, or alcohol (major narcissistic crisis), the addict has to shift dependency to a person, an ideal, or to the procedure itself of the cure.

26 . 27

Discipline and addiction. Practice your scales. Repetitions. Bach on coffee. Berlioz on hallucinogens (but also on coffee and cigars): The Witches' Sabbath, a concoction of *Faust* and the opium dreams that Berlioz read in De Quincey's *Confessions of an English Opium Eater*. Mussorgsky's wine, Stravinsky's cigarettes.

28 . 29

Drugs are excentric. They are animated by an outside already inside. Endorphins relate internal secretion to the external chemical.

Drugs are excentric and depropriative. In "Hashish in Marseilles," Benjamin, citing "his" experience with hashish, borrows from Baudelaire his opening.

PRELIMINARY REMARK: *One of the first signs that hashish is beginning to take effect "is a dull feeling of foreboding; something strange, ineluctable is approaching . . . the subject is surprised and overwhelmed. His laughter, all his utterances happen to him like outward events."*

Benjamin takes an injection of a foreign body (Baudelaire's *Les Paradis artificiels*) in order to express his inner experience. This is by no means an atypical gesture. To locate "his" ownmost subjectivity, Thomas De Quincey cited Wordsworth. These texts are on each other. A textual communication based on *tropium.*

30 . 31

At about the same time as Romanticism turned it into the seriousness of *oeuvre,* literature initiated the experience of its own substance: organized by a concept of work, it soon came to know play's gravity. Such gravity exposed the work to experiences of peril and experimentation, obligating literature to map out a toxicogeography—an imaginary place where literature could crash against its abysses and float amid fragments of residual transcendency. The engagement with its essence threw literature off any predictably legible course but also created the mirage of a genuine autonomy.

In *Annäherungen: Drogen und Rausch,* Ernst Jünger, who had turned Heidegger on to technology, writes about the drug-drive. While he begins to ask how the prosthetic subject is constituted, his thought is not all that remote from what Benjamin writes on hashish, or even De Quincey on opium. It sometimes resembles Marguerite Duras's alcoholizations: this is a saturated text, pushing beyond the materiality of the book, though not into any ideality. Drugs, for which Jünger effectively writes a manifesto, are the site of an allotechnology: technology's intimate other, sharing the same project as historical *dés-oeuvrement.* Jünger explores the right to drugs as well as the supplementary interiority that they produce. It is widely alleged in Freiburg that the "philosopher" with whom Jünger drops acid is Martin Heidegger.

Jünger's version of the Narcissus myth poses the relation of narcissism and drugs as a problem of *Sehnsucht* (Longing/Desire). But where Narcissus's dilemma involves the commonplace disjunction between erotism and knowledge—"How can I 'know' myself?"—drugs open up the gulf of extra-erotic, extra-epistemic desire.

The communication systems with the question concerning addiction are on. Each time they beam different signals, along edges of new interiorities. Much like the paradigms installed by the discovery of endorphins, Being-on-drugs indicates that a structure is already in place, prior to the production of that materiality we call drugs, including virtual reality or cyberprojections. Our problem remains how to present a logic of something that is already there without resorting to the ontic. One of the implicit questions to emerge in this probe unavoidably concerns technology and, in Heidegger's terms, *Gestell.* What is *Gestell* in relation to the addictive hankering of Dasein? Would it not require remodeling in light of Dasein's revision according to what in English is persistently translated as "hankering" and "addiction"? Heidegger possibilizes Dasein's internalization of *Gestell* according to the chemical prosthesis. It appears that he thought about addiction (in *Being and Time,* in *Schelling's Treatise on the Essence of Human Freedom*), but not about the specificity of the technology of the drug. Yet, addicted Dasein has everything to do with *Gestell.* Whereas in his work on *Gestell* Heidegger indicates man's blind dependency on technology in this phase of metaphysical disclosure, in his fundamental ontology there is a reading of "hooked pulsion" (*der Drang*) and dependency (*Nachhängen*). In pure pulsion, anxiety has not yet become free, he argues, while in dependency anxiety is still bound. The question arises as an existential-ontological fundamental phenomenon that, Heidegger admonishes, is hardly simple in its structure ("in seiner Struktur nicht einfach ist"). The larger issues of will, urge, and craving belong to the question of care. To understand the extent to which care is implicated in these structures, we need to zoom in on a regional mapping of Dasein's dependency.

At one point in *Being and Time* Heidegger puts his rhetoric on tranquilizers. This occurs when concern, in its average everydayness, becomes blind to its possibilities "and tranquillizes itself with that which is merely 'actual'" ("Das Sein des Daseins als Sorge," "Dasein's Being as Care" §41). In a gesture of stepping back that is characteristic of his thought, he asserts: "This tranquilizing does not rule out a high degree of diligence in one's concerns, but arouses it." The tranquilizer of *Sorge* acts as a stimulant, if only eventually to argue that Dasein closes off essential possibilities when it is shown to be addicted. For Heidegger's rhetoric of drugs is, as it were, injected into the very place where *Being and Time* treats the problem of dependency. It turns out that when Dasein "sinks into an addiction," there is not merely an addiction present-at-hand, "but the entire structure of care has been modified." This modification involves nothing less than locating the threat that addiction poses to Being. Heidegger places addiction close to willing and to wishing. Dasein's Being reveals itself as care. If we are to work out this basic existential phenomenon, we must distinguish it from phenomena which might be proximally identified with care, such as will, wish, addiction, and urge. Care cannot be derived from these, since they themselves are founded upon it ("The Question of the Primordial Totality of Dasein's Structural Whole" §39).

Now, anxiousness as a state of mind is for Heidegger a fundamental way of Being-in-the-world. As one of Dasein's possibilities of Being, anxiety—together with Dasein itself as disclosed in it—provides the phenomenal basis for "explicitly grasping Dasein's primordial totality of Being" (§ 39). One could say that, according to this reading, anxiety is absolutely necessary for the possibility of Being-free, and that tranquilizing effects menace the integrity of care itself, which is the primordial structural totality: "Being-free for one's ownmost potentiality-for-Being, and therewith for the possibility of authenticity and inauthenticity, is shown, with a primordial, elemental concreteness, in anxiety" (§41). In pure urge, care has not yet become free, though care makes it possible for Dasein to be urged on by itself. In addiction, however, care has always been bound (§41)—Being-in-the-world is in its entirety crucially modified. The passage in which Heidegger interprets addiction warrants substantial citation. At the same time, we are in a sense "dropping" Heidegger in a complicated movement of withdrawal that consists in swallowing a full passage:

> The phenomenon of care in its totality is essentially something that cannot be torn asunder; so any attempts to trace it back to special acts or drives like willing and wishing or urge and addiction, or to construct it out of these, will be unsuccessful.
>
> Willing and wishing are rooted with ontological necessity in Dasein as care; they are not just ontologically undifferentiated Experiences occurring in a 'stream' which is completely indefinite with regard to the meaning of its Being. This is no less the case with urge and addiction. These too are grounded in care in so far as they can be exhibited in Dasein at all. This does not prevent them from being ontologically constitutive even for entities that merely 'live.' But the basic ontological state of 'living' is a problem in its own right and can be tackled only reductively and privately in terms of the ontology of Dasein.
>
> Care is ontologically 'earlier' than the phenomena we have just mentioned, which admittedly can, within certain limits, always be 'described' appropriately without our needing to have the full ontological horizon visible, or even to be familiar with it at all. From the standpoint of our present investigation in fundamental ontology, which aspires neither

to a thematically complete ontology of Dasein nor even to a concrete anthropology, it must suffice to suggest how these phenomena are grounded existentially in care. . . . The average everydayness of concern becomes blind to its possibilities, and tranquillizes itself with that which is merely 'actual.' This tranquillizing does not rule out a high degree of diligence in one's concern, but arouses it. In this case no positive new possibilities are willed, but that which is at one's disposal becomes 'tactically' altered in such a way that there is a semblance of something happening.

All the same, this tranquillized 'willing' under the guidance of the "they," does not signify that one's Being towards one's potentiality-for-Being has been extinguished, but only that it has been modified. In such a case, one's Being towards possibilities shows itself for the most part as mere *wishing*. In the wish Dasein projects its Being upon possibilities which not only have not been taken hold of in concern, but whose fulfilment has not even been pondered over and expected. On the contrary, in the mode of mere wishing, the ascendancy of Being-ahead-of-oneself brings with it a lack of understanding for the factical possibilities. When the world has been primarily projected as a wish-world, Being-in-the-world has lost itself inertly in what is at its disposal; but it has done so in such a way that, in light of what is wished for, that which is at its disposal (and this is all that is ready-to-hand) is never enough. Wishing is an existential modification of projecting oneself understandingly, when such self-understanding has fallen forfeit to thrownness and just keeps *hankering* after possibilities. Such hankering (*Nachhängen*) *closes off* the possibilities; what is 'there' in wishful hankering turns into the 'actual world.' Ontologically, wishing presupposes care.

In hankering, Being-already-alongside . . . takes priority. The "ahead-of-itself-in-Being-already-in . . ." is correspondingly modified. Dasein's hankering as it falls makes manifest its *addiction* to becoming 'lived' by whatever world it is in. This addiction shows the character of Being out for something [*Ausseins auf*. . .]. Being-ahead-of-oneself has lost itself in a 'just-always-already-alongside' [*Nur-immer-schon-bei*]. What one is addicted 'towards' [*Das "Hin-zu" des Hanges*] is to let oneself be drawn by the sort of thing for which the addiction hankers. If Dasein, as it were, sinks into an addiction then there is not merely an addiction present-at-hand, but the entire structure of care has been modified. Dasein has become blind, and puts all possibility into the service of the addiction.

On the other hand, the *urge* 'to live' is something 'towards' which one is impelled, and it brings the impulsion along with it of its own accord. It is 'towards this at any price.' The urge seeks to crowd out [*verdrängen*] other possibilities. Here too the Being-ahead-of-oneself is one that is inauthentic, even if one is assailed by an urge coming from the very thing that is urging one on. The urge can outrun one's current state of mind and one's understanding. But then Dasein is not—and never is—a 'mere urge' to which other kinds of controlling or guiding behaviour are added from time to time; rather, as a modification of the entirety of Being-in-the-world, it is always care already.

In pure urge, care has not yet become free, though care first makes it ontologically possible for Dasein to be urged on by itself. In addiction, however, care has always been bound. Addiction and urge are possibilities rooted in the thrownness of Dasein. There urge 'to live' is not to be annihilated; the addiction to becoming 'lived' by the world is not to be rooted out. But because these are both grounded ontologically in care, and only because of this, they are both to be modified in an ontical and existentiel manner by care—by care as something authentic. (*Being and Time,* trans. John Macquarrie and Edward Robinson [New York: Harper & Row: 1962], pp.194–96).

What motivates this strategic move on dependency? Having established ontologically this crucial state-of-mind, Heidegger now has to protect anxiety from the contagious drift of its proximate others. Anxiety has to be assured some clarity because, as one of Dasein's possibilities of Being, it supplies the phenomenal basis for "explicitly grasping Dasein's primordial totality of Being." In order to designate with exactitude the way Dasein's Being reveals itself, that is, as *care,* Heidegger must ascertain that parasitical phenomena such as urge and addiction are at once named and crowded out. While these phenomena cannot be derived from but originate in care, they nonetheless display the problematic powers of being ontologically constitutive in certain cases. Heidegger cannot allow the family of wishing and willing, addiction and urge, to bust the primordial structural totality which care guarantees. Thus, the phenomenon of care resists disunification; it is "essentially something that cannot be torn asunder," and Heidegger blocks efforts to trace care back to special acts or drives which include addiction. At the same time, Heidegger appears to be granting addiction a distinct status when he rejects the ontological potion that merely would blend the Experience of addiction with willing and wishing. Claims can be made for the meaning of the Being of addiction when Heidegger links it to the ground of caring: "they are not just ontologically undifferentiated Experiences occurring in a 'stream' which is completely indefinite with regard to the meaning of its Being."

The discussion of care tinctured by addiction obliges Heidegger to encounter a limit in his 'description' of fundamental ontology, for it is in these passages that he repeatedly marks the incompletion of a certain level of unfolding. When arguing the case of addiction and urge, he writes that "these too are grounded in care in so far as they can be exhibited in Dasein at all." Addiction evades presentation, working itself out in a mode of secrecy, which makes it somewhat difficult for Dasein to display signs of addiction. Exposed, Dasein cannot expose the urges that have invaded it according to any classical protocol of presentability. Just as Dasein has to cover itself up, *Being and Time* signals a needed expository retreat at this place: "neither . . . a thematically complete ontology of Dasein nor even a concrete anthropology, it must suffice." This withdrawal, however, points precisely to the problem of the addicted Dasein which cannot and yet must say, as Heidegger will argue, "it must suffice."

When his argument obliges him to focus on "this tranquilized 'willing'", Heidegger takes recourse to the metaphysically laden term, "projection": "In the wish Dasein projects its Being . . . ." Now, the class of special acts including wishing and addiction appears to be temporally on the run, promoting the ascendancy of Being-ahead-of-oneself. This class has desired and projected possibilities that have not gradually grown from a ground of concern and whose fulfillment has not been submitted to the patient tapping of thought. The fulfillment of a drive such as addiction cannot be truly projected. While it responds to the immediacy of a demand, it arrives as a surprise attack: a hit ("whose fulfillment has not even been pondered over and expected"). Being on the run, addiction dumps understanding along the way, the way one flushes evidence when there's a bust. Or worse still, the addicted Dasein "brings with it a lack of understanding," as if this lack were added to Dasein. While Dasein is on the run and ahead-of-itself without time to think, Being-in-the-world has lost itself in inertia because it is bound only to what is at its disposal. This is where Being-in-the-world encounters radical insufficiency as it begins to close off real possibilities for itself.

For while it loses itself in all that is ready-to-hand (whatever is at its disposal), Being-in-the-world discovers that all this is never enough. Still, it doesn't let go but increases the level of dependency (*Nachhängen*) in a kind of vertigo of endless repetition. At the same time desperate for more, Being-in-the-world experiences through addiction the self-sufficiency of what is "in" the world in the most desolate sense. You can only be addicted to what is available, which is what traps you in a circle without futurity: you're stuck Being-already-alongside and when Dasein needs a fix as it falls it lets itself be lived by whatever world it is in. Thus Being-ahead-of-oneself, which nonetheless had a temporal and necessary advantage, lapses into a 'just-always-already-alongside'—an ontological way of saying "going nowhere fast," except that the pace is slowed down because this Dasein has been sped up only to fall behind.

Heidegger does not name the object that would respond materially to the call of addiction but suggests that addiction is itself addicted: "What one is addicted 'towards' is to let oneself be drawn by the sort of thing for which the addiction hankers." What is this sort of thing? Heidegger leaves options open—it could be any opiate, including figures, agents or other exigencies of ecstasy such as love, but also including the political drug of a German "destiny." Detached from the strictly determined referent, addiction can also hanker after a mystified communion of community, a mythology of "Volk" or even economy, which is why one is also susceptible to becoming intoxicated with any regime of reunification. Dasein, as he writes, becomes blind, and puts all possibilities into the service of addiction. Addiction is imperious. But there is still another hand.

On the other hand, while downshifting from addiction

to urge, Heidegger nonetheless connects these to a certain life principle, for the issue settles on nothing less than "the *urge* 'to live,'" which is something 'towards' which one is impelled. This impulsion reveals a type of autonomy and necessity because it comes of its own accord. The problem lies in the relentlessness of the impulsion, for the urge is programmed for mobilization "at any price." The urge is imperialistic and follows a regime of repression, crowding out all other possibilities. While the urging on of the urge belongs to vitality, and thus to a more positive structure than addicted addiction, less passive and debilitated, it too offers an inauthentic mode of Being-ahead-of-oneself: "The urge can outrun one's current state-of-mind and one's understanding." The urge darts out from a particular rhythm that Dasein needs in order to keep up with its understanding, and while Dasein is ruled by a movement of constant deferral of mastery, this flash of outrunning is going too far. But there is yet another constraint upon Dasein.

If Dasein is supposed to care always already, pure urge can intervene only as a deviancy that would tie Dasein up. Care first makes it ontologically possible for Dasein to be urged on by itself; yet pure urge restrains care, making it susceptible to unfreedom. In a sense, freedom depends upon Dasein's openness to anxiety which addiction and urge are seen to divert. Dasein needs to follow a type of repetition that is not burdened with compulsion in the original sense of the term—i.e., as *Zwang,* force or coercion. And yet, Dasein's trajectory often mirrors addictive compulsion and the extreme submission to an experience of fascination and guilt. Thrownness is an experience of nothing or nullity, an experience which Heidegger calls "guilt"—a radical impotence regarding the conditions of the "there" in which one finds oneself thrown. In thrownness, the experience of Being-possible is an experience of total powerlessness—powerlessness or fascination, or heady vertigo. In anxiety, Dasein is taken back fully to its sheer uncanniness, and hit with vertigo (*BT*, 344). But this rush gives Dasein its thrownness as something possible, and as something that can be repeated. However, it gives Dasein repeatability as something that can be taken up in a resolution (*Entschluss*) in Being-toward-death. Thrownness happens to a radically passive Dasein which is nonetheless somehow granted the impulsion to repeat this thrownness. At once passive and equipped with the impetus to repeat, Dasein still has to be prevented from falling into empty repetition compulsion. Dasein acts upon itself, Heidegger suggests, spontaneously, out of its own Being-guilty, and thereby discloses this Being-guilty as a possibility that may be acted upon. Dasein lives constantly with anxiety—Heidegger underscores the fact that anxiety is accompanied by understanding, and this may be one reason why the suppression of anxiety by mirror-forms and accelerators, its artificial additives, poses a threat to a kind of affirmative instability of Dasein. For Dasein must assume its thrownness and affirm it through an uncompelled yet necessary repetition. One might hazard that Dasein needs to face its intoxication—fascination and vertigo—soberly, that is, with the tensed fist of anxiety. That's why Dasein is split over where to go: it is drawn toward the experience of fascination and passivity even as it is drawn (or draws itself) toward the experience of death.

Of course, the same could be said of the suicidal rush of the addicted Dasein. Except that the addicted Dasein doesn't detach itself from the experience of passivity in order to *decide* upon repetition in time; rather, it is inhabited by a compulsion that blindly bypasses finitude's markers. Heidegger may not say it quite this way, but he does go to the trouble of protecting Dasein from making a habit of addiction, urge, wishing and tranquilized 'willing,' as he puts it. He will do it again in other works, as when he himself injects tranquilizers into the Nietzschean corpus in order to subdue the ravages of *Rausch* (intoxication). At other times, however, Heidegger appears to turn towards a structure of addiction as the exemplary way by which the desire to hear (*hören*) is installed in the destiny of a little boy (*What Is Called Thinking?* Lecture V). Dasein is always exposed to the possibility of Being-addicted, not because it is weak or hungry (Dasein has never been seen eating, as both Levinas and Derrida have observed) but because addiction discloses a moment in care's responsiveness, from which it is derived, and possibly locates itself between the Experience of impotence and Being-toward-death.

What addiction does block in *Being and Time*—and on this point Heidegger is very clear—is the opening for which anxiety is properly responsible. Such an opening is granted by the notions of freedom and decision, for freedom is maintained only in and through anxiety. When Heidegger accents the possibility of decision, Dasein emerges victorious—free to construct a monument to its agony by which it reverently preserves the existence-that-has-been-there. Here addiction threatens Dasein's memory bank with a series of hold-ups that depletes existence down to what is ready-to-hand. Dasein is no longer free to make the decision to decide, condemning itself rather to perpetual irresolution.

§

There is one more twist to Heidegger's argument which should not be left by the wayside. Freedom decides for decision and decidability. But true freedom involves the freedom to choose what is good *and* what is bad; and decision, if it is within decision that freedom emerges, has to decide for good or evil. Dasein, for its part, may never quite cut it, may never accomplish the freedom of which it is in principle capable. To a certain extent, Dasein has always committed an already "bad" act because it does not exist according to its ownmost possibility for existence; it has not absolutely given itself over to the world—it is not yet liberated, so to speak, because it keeps falling short of the generosity of Being. The question that *Being and Time* leaves with us—which will be our opening—is this: if one can decide for destruction, and if this possibility is inscribed in the very Being of existence, does not such a decision also destroy decision in its *existentiell* essence?

This is a question Jean-Luc Nancy elaborates in *L'Expérience de la liberté,* a question whose major resonances we have to seek in a literature of destructive *jouissance.* But as Nancy also makes clear, *freedom is not a question* but an absolute given, a fact—a kind of liberality, then, that offers itself as a generosity more original still than any single instance of freedom.

We, for our part, have serious and urgent choices before us: to begin with what is given, to urge an ethics of decision that would not be merely negative or defensive.

PART TWO : TOWARD A NARCOANALYSIS

This work does not accord with literary criticism in the traditional sense. Yet it is devoted to the understanding of a literary work. It could be said to reside within the precincts of philosophical endeavor. Indeed, it tries to understand an object that splits existence into incommensurable articulations. This object resists the revelation of its truth to the point of retaining the status of absolute otherness. Nonetheless, it has given rise to laws and moral pronouncements. This fact, in itself, is not alarming. The problem is signaled elsewhere, in the exhaustion of language. Where might one go today, to what source can one turn, in order to activate a just constativity? We no longer see in philosophy the ultimate possibilities for knowing the limits of human experience.[5] And yet we began this study by citing Nietzsche. There were two reasons for this selection. In the first place, Nietzsche was the philosopher to think with his body, to "dance," which is a nice way of saying also to convulse, even to retch. And then, Nietzsche was the one to put out the call for a supramoral imperative.[6] This summons in itself will urge us on—for we are dealing in a way with the youngest vice, still very immature, still often misjudged and taken for something else, still hardly aware of itself . . .

What follows, then, is essentially a work on *Madame Bovary,* and nothing more. If it were another type of work—in the genre of philosophical essay, psychoanalytic interpretation, or political analysis—it would be expected to make certain kinds of assertions which obey a whole grammar of procedure and certitudes. The prestige and historical recommendation of those methods of inquiry would have secured the project within a tolerably reliable frame. However, it is too soon to say with certainty that one has fully understood how to conduct the study of addiction and, in particular, how it may bear upon drugs. To understand in such a way would be to stop reading, to close the book, as it were, or even to throw the book at someone.

I cannot say that I am prepared to take sides on this exceedingly difficult issue, particularly when the sides have been drawn with such conceptual awkwardness. Clearly, it is as preposterous to be "for" drugs as it is to take up a position "against" drugs. Provisionally they may be comprehended as master objects of considerable libidinal investment, whose essence still remains to be determined. As it happens, literature is on drugs and about drugs—and here I retain the license to open the semantic range of this term (which does not even amount to concept). I shall come back to the many fluctuations of meaning and usage in the course of my argument. For the present, "drugs" can be understood to involve materially (1) products of a natural origin, often known in antiquity; (2) products evolved from modern pharmaceutical chemistry; and (3) parapharmacological substances, or products prepared by and for the addict.[7] This says nothing as yet for the symbolic values of drugs, their rootedness in ritual and the sacred, their promise of exteriority, the technological extension of supernatural structures, or the spaces carved out in the imaginary by the introduction of a chemical prosthesis.

Under the impacted signifier of drugs, America is fighting a war against a number of felt intrusions. They have to do mostly with the drift and contagion of a foreign substance, or of what is revealed as foreign (even if it should be homegrown). Like any good parasite, drugs travel both inside and outside of the boundaries of a narcissistically defended politics. They double for the values with which they are at odds, thus haunting and reproducing the capital market, creating visionary expansions, producing a lexicon of body control and a private property of self—all of which awaits review.

Drugs resist conceptual arrest. No one has thought to define them in their essence, which is not to say "they" do not exist. On the contrary. Everywhere dispensed, in one form or another, their strength lies in their virtual and fugitive patterns. They do not close forces with an external enemy (the easy way out) but have a secret communications network with the internalized demon. Something is beaming out signals, calling drugs home.[8]

The complex identity of this substance, which is never as such a substance, has given rise to the inscription of a shameful history. This is not the place to trace its intricate contours, for it is an open history whose approach routes are still blocked; nonetheless, the necessity of pursuing such an endeavor still stands. On some level of thinking's probity it is either entirely self-canceling or far too *easy* to treat drugs. Precisely because they are everywhere and can be made to do, or undo, or promise, anything. They participate in the analysis of the broken word, or a history of warfare: methedrine, or methyl-amphetamine, synthesized in Germany, had a determining effect in Hitler's Blitzkrieg; heroin comes from *heroisch,** and Göring never went anywhere without his supply; Dr. Hubertus Strughold, father of space medicine, conducted mescaline exper-

*In fact, heroin was first produced in 1874 at St Mary's Hospital in London. It was reinvented or "discovered" in Germany in the 1890s and marketed by Bayer under the trade name "heroin," which derives from *heroisch* (cf. Virginia Berridge and Griffith Edwards, *Opium and the People* [New Haven and London: Yale University Press, 1987], p.xx).

iments at Dachau—indeed, it would be difficult to dissociate drugs from a history of modern warfare and genocide. One could begin perhaps in the contiguous neighborhood of the ethnocide of the American Indian by alcohol or strategic viral infection, and then one could never end . . .

The contagious spread of the entity described as drugs is discursively manifest. Drugs cannot be placed securely within the frontiers of traditional disciplines: anthropology, biology, chemistry, politics, medicine, or law, could not, solely on the strength of their respective epistemologies, claim to contain or counteract them. While everywhere dealt with, drugs act as a radically nomadic parasite let loose from the will of language.

While they resist *presentation,* drugs are still too readily appropriable. One problem dragging down thought is that the drug wars might scan well with the present atmosphere of consensual reading. It is actually becoming impolite to enter areas of conflict.[9] Anyone who has not been prudent in thinking through this fragile zone where nonknowledge dominates knowledge has in any case been burned.

I refer in particular to the professional history of Sigmund Freud who, for the sake of some unplumbable purpose, staked his early career entirely on cocaine and on the essays devoted to cocaine. As a result of *Über Coca*—this text and the subsequent defense, "Remarks on Craving for and Fear of Cocaine," are not included in the *Standard Edition of the Complete Psychological Works*—Freud was publicly reprimanded and privately assailed. Why he willfully ignored the underside of cocaine usage researched by Dr. Louis Lewin, shall have to maintain its status as enigma. His altogether favorable disposition toward cocaine (he recommended it for combating fatigue, against aging, as a local anaesthetic) earned him the published reproof of the famous Berlin psychiatrist, Albrecht Erlenmeyer.[10] Such attacks upon his scientific integrity for promoting the cause of cocaine might have cost a lesser ego its destiny. The personal aspect of disaster brought about by this impassioned research concerned his intimate friend, Von Fleischl, who was the first morphine addict to be treated by cocaine: our first European cocaine addict. Freud attended his friend through a night of paranoid terror, where he witnessed the felt invasion and devouring of Von Fleischl by endless insects and tireless demons. At great cost to himself, his friends, and his father (who was treated with cocaine by his son's prescription), Freud may have discovered something about the toxic drive that could not obtain immediate clearance. In his own work, the cocaine drama broke the ground for the study of hysterical neurosis.

If anything, Freud serves here as a warning system. He never, it seems to me, shook the trouble that cocaine advocacy earned him. This is not the place to analyze that fatal encounter, nor certainly would it be appropriate to concoct foolish moralizations as if one already understood what addiction is all about. There are good and bad addictions, and anything can serve the function of a drug. "Drugs," in any case, make us face the gaping chasms of *Beyond the Pleasure Principle,* where death drive and desire round up their victims.

In his more restrained estimations, Freud has characterized the addict as evoking the charm of cats and birds of prey with their inaccessibility, their apparent libidinal autonomy.[11] This is not very far from his description, in another context, of women. (The place where the addict meets the feminine in a desperate attempt at social renarcissization is carefully marked in *Madame Bovary.*) Narcissistic withdrawal equally introduces a scandalous figure into the society of humans by removing the addicted subject from the sphere of human connectibility. But perhaps the hint of libidinal autonomy, or what Félix Guattari describes as "the second degree of solitude," furnishes the most menacing among social attributes.[12] Jacques Lacan appears to confirm the conviction that drug addiction belongs to the domain of a post-analytical era reserved perhaps for schizoanalysis and the like; indeed, he sees the addict as constituting a hopeless subject of psychoanalysis: "Addiction (*la toxicomanie*) opens a field where no single word of the subject is reliable, and where he escapes analysis altogether."[13] This is giving up quickly. William Burroughs shares quite the same opinion from the other side of experience: "Morphine addiction is a metabolic illness brought about by the use of morphine. In my opinion psychological treatment is not only useless it is contraindicated."[14] A collusion on the parts of Lacan and Burroughs does not mean, however, that the psychotreatability of the addict is wholly out of the question, or that psychoanalysis would offer a useless or archaic access code for unlocking the whole problem. For, to the extent that addiction was at one point within the jurisdiction of *jouissance*—indeed, we are dealing with an epidemic of misfired *jouissance*—the major pusher, the one who gave the orders to shoot up, was surely the superego. In order to urge this point with some sustainment of clarity we shall have to enter the clinic of phantasms that Flaubert chose to call *Madame Bovary*.

The modern history of the attempt to stabilize a definition of drugs comprises long, dense, and contradictory moments (Queen Victoria waged war twice, for instance, in order to ensure the free commerce of opium).* The

*Involved in the Indian opium trade with China, Britain fought two "opium wars" against China, in 1839–42 and again in 1856–58.

legal history of drugs compels analyses of the means by which drugs have been enlisted to erode the American criminal justice system. Airports now establish the clearest rhetorical space for reading the consequences of what Justice Brennan had once projected as the "unanalyzed exercise of judicial will."[15] State control towers have effected the merger between air and drug traffic, instituting the airport as a premonitory law-free zone where the subject's orifices are kept open to investigation. No probable cause is necessary here. *Droit de la drogue,* a significant French study of the problem, clarifies the prohibitionist spell under which America continues to conduct its interventions.[16] The study does not fail to analyze the effects of the xenophobic, racist and economic calculations that have commanded moral, legal, and military discourses. Its theoretical propositions derive from constructions concerning the freedom of the legal subject and his right to be protected from the condition of enslavement that drugs are said unavoidably to produce. It is a matter of determining at what point the object takes possession of the subject. We shall leave these terms to flood their undeconstructed history.

I can make no pretense to possessing legal competence more elaborate than that of any literate person. I would suggest only that one consider the degree to which the literary object has itself been treated juridically as a drug. In one case it fell to the favor of the literary work to be handled as a medicinal substance, possibly indeed by an "unconscious" legal manipulation. This is the case of James Joyce's *Ulysses,* where the work's fate was considerably advantaged by its classification as emetic function rather than as pornographic inducement. These were the terms upon which it was performatively granted entry rights into the U.S. Be that as it may, *Ulysses,* whether legally conceived as emetic formula or as aphrodisiac philtre, was in the first place distilled down to its essence as a drug.

Naked Lunch evinces a similar collapse of the boundary between obscenity and drugs. In *Attorney General* v. *A Book Named "Naked Lunch,"* the court finds the following:

> The Supreme Court of the United States has held that, to justify a holding of obscenity, "three elements must coalesce: it must be established that (a) the dominant theme of the material taken as a whole appeals to a prurient interest in sex; (b) the material is patently offensive because it affronts contemporary community standards . . . and (c) the material is *utterly* without redeeming social value [emphasis supplied]; *A Book Named "Johns Cleland's Memoirs of a Woman of Pleasure"* v. *Attorney General of Mass.* 383 U.S. 413, 418–421. . . . As to whether [*Naked Lunch*] has any redeeming social value, the record contains many reviews and articles in literary and other publications discussing seriously this controversial book portraying the hallucinations of a drug addict. Thus it appears that a substantial and intelligent group in the community believes the book to be of some literary significance.[17]

The slippage from obscenity to the representation of hallucination—in other words, the representation of representation—cannot fail to raise questions about the veilings that both literature and drugs cast. This order of questioning had already penetrated to the case of *Madame Bovary,* where it was held that the curtain of non-representation (the carriage scene) exploded hallucinatory rage in the open space of the socius. The menace of literature in these cases consists in its pointing to what is not there in any ordinary sense of ontological unveiling. The court is not wrong to institute the proximity of hallucination and obscenity as neighboring territorialities, since both put in question the power of literature to veil its insight or to limit its exposure. Literature is most exposed when it stops representing, that is, when it ceases veiling itself with the excess that we commonly call *meaning*.

The question comes down to the way literature dresses up the wound of its non-being when it goes out into the world. On this point, the cases of *Madame Bovary* and *Naked Lunch* are only to a certain degree different (it is all a matter of dosage), but the matter of representation continues to be the same: the court keeps a close watch on creatures of the simulacrum.

There can be no doubt about it. *Naked Lunch* gets out of trouble only when the social veil of literary review has been thrown over it. Literature has to be seen wearing something external to itself, it cannot simply circulate its non-being, and almost any article will do. This would affirm at least one value of the book review as that legal force which covers up the work.

§

Well, then. It is not so much a question of scientific knowledge. Nor certainly can it be a question of confidence in writing. There are certain things that force your hand. You find yourself incontrovertibly obligated: something occurs prior to owing, and more fundamental still than that of which any trace of empirical guilt can give an account. This relation—to whom? to what?—is no more and no less than your liability—what you owe before you think, understand, or give; that is, what you owe from the very fact that you exist, before you can properly owe. You do not have to *do* anything about your liability, and most finitudes don't. Still, it copilots your every move, planning your every flight, and it remains the place shadowed by the infinite singularity of your finitude.

The obligation that can force your hand resembles something of a historial compulsion: you are compelled to respond to a situation which has never as such been addressed to you, where you can do no more than run into an identificatory impasse. Nonetheless, you find yourself rising to the demand, as if the weight of justice depended upon your inconsequential advance.

It did not seem advantageous to put at risk the peculiar idiom of this work by installing ethical tonalities that may in the end correspond only weakly to its critical punch (Flaubert: "The worth of a book can be judged by the strength of the punches it gives and the length of time it takes you to recover from them.").[18] The task of producing an introduction made me hesitate, the way a translator hesitates over the prospects of a sacrificial economy that will nevertheless dominate the entire work. Might as well face it: Some hesitations are rigorous. They own up to the fact that no decision is strictly possible without the experience of the undecidable. To the extent that one may no longer be simply guided—by Truth, by light or logos—decisions have to be made. Yet I wanted neither to protect Emma B. from what was about to happen (she had to remain exposed) nor to pervert her further. I certainly did not want to create a disposable limit, an explanatory phase that, at lift off, could easily fall behind. This would have come too close to repeating a structure of dejection with which drugs have been associated—a structure where there is neither introjection nor even incorporation, but which posits the body as the no-return of disposability: the trash-body, pivoted on its own excrementality. Doubling for the remainder, however, this moment in my argument would occupy the terrifying position of quasi-transcendence because it can be made to determine the value of the inside from which it is ejected. And yet, one is liable, and one has to find a way of thinking this liability as if one were concluding an affirmative contract with an endlessly demanding alterity.

More so perhaps than any other "substance," whether real or imagined, drugs thematize the dissociation of autonomy and responsibility that has marked our epoch since Kant. Despite the indeterminacy and heterogeneity that characterize these phenomena, drugs are crucially related to the question of freedom. Kant himself devotes pages of the *Anthropology* to contemplating the values of civic strength as they are affected by intoxicating foods (under which he comprehended mushrooms, wild rosemary, acanthus, Peruvian chicha, the South Sea Island's ava, and opium). The questions attending drugs disclose only a moment in the history of addiction. As such, drugs have accrued a meager hermeneutics in proportion to a considerable mobilization of force.

No one has so much as defined drugs, and this is in part because they are non-theorizable. Still, they have globalized a massive instance of destructive *jouissance,* they assert desire's mutation within a post-analytic phrasing, or put another way, drugs name the exposition of our modernity to the incompletion of *jouissance.* Perhaps the quality of these stakes explains in part why they have become the elusive objects of planetary warfare at the very moment when "democracy" is on the rebound. The intersecting cut between freedom, drugs and the addicted condition (what we are symptomatologizing as "Being-on-drugs") deserves an interminable analysis whose heavily barred doors can be no more than cracked open by a solitary research.

Narcotic desire's implications for freedom did not entirely escape Kant's gaze (hence the need for prescriptions in general). But it was not until Thomas De Quincey that drugs were pushed toward a philosophy of decision. The

Confessions of an English Opium Eater can be shown to perturb an entire ontology by having drugs participate in a movement of unveiling that is capable of discovering no prior or more fundamental ground. Unveiling and unclouding, opium, on De Quincey's account, brings the higher faculties into a kind of legal order, an absolute legislative harmony. If it perturbs ontology this is in order to institute something else. The ontological revision which it undertakes would not be subject to the regime of *alèthia,* or rather, the clarity which opium urges is not dependent upon a prior unveiling. Where the warring parts of the *Confessions* refuse to suture, one detects the incredible scars of decision. Always a recovering addict, Kant's subject was not particularly pathological in the pursuit of his habits; De Quincey's addict has been exposed to another limit of experience, to the promise of exteriority. Offering a discreet if spectacular way out, an atopical place of exit, drugs forced *decision* upon the subject.

Self-dissolving and regathering, the subject became linked to the possibility of a new autonomy, and opium illuminated in this case (Baudelaire, though under De Quincey's influence, was to use it differently) an individual who finally could not identify with his ownmost autonomy but found himself instead subjected to heroic humiliation in the regions of the sublime. Opium became the transparency upon which one could review the internal conflict of freedom, the cleave of subjectivity where it encounters the abyss of destructive *jouissance.*

The ever-dividing self was transported on something other than the sacred, though the effects of revelation were not unrelated. Decisions would have to be met, one had to become a master strategist in the ceaseless war against pain. The most striking aspect of De Quincey's decision resides in the fact that it resists regulation by a telos of knowledge. To this end his elaboration has uncovered for us a critical structure of decision to the extent that it has been tinctured by non-knowledge, based largely upon a state of anarchivization.[19] This leaves any future thinking of drugs, if this should be possible, in the decidedly fragile position of system abandonment. There is no system that can presently hold or take "drugs" for long. Instituted on the basis of moral or political evaluations, the concept of drugs cannot be comprehended under any independent, scientific system.

These observations do not mean to imply that a certain type of narcotic supplement has been in the least rejected by metaphysics. To a great degree, it is all more or less a question of dosage (as Nietzsche said of history). Precisely due to the promise of exteriority which they are thought to extend, drugs have been redeemed by the conditions of transcendency and revelation with which they are not uncommonly associated. But qualities such as these are problematic because they tend to maintain drugs on "this side" of a thinking of experience. Sacralized or satanized, when our politics and theories prove still to be under God's thumb, they install themselves as codependents; ever recycling the transcendental trace of freedom, they have been the undaunted suppliers of a metaphysical craving.

There can be no doubt about it. What is required is a genuine ethics of decision. But this in turn calls for a still higher form of drug.

§

Madame Bovary I daresay is about bad drugs. Equally, it is about thinking we have properly understood them. But if the novel matches its reputation for rendering its epoch—our modernity—intelligible, then we would do well to recall that *epoch* also means interruption, arrest, suspension and, above all, suspension of judgment.[20] *Madame Bovary* travels the razor's edge of understanding/reading protocols. In this context understanding is given as something that happens when you are no longer reading. It is not the open-ended Nietzschean echo, "Have I been understood?" but rather the "I understand" that means you have ceased suspending judgment over a chasm of the real. Out of this collapse of judgment no genuine decision can be allowed to emerge. Madame Bovary understood too much; she understood what things were supposed to be like and suffered a series of ethical injuries for this certitude. Her understanding made her legislate closure at every step of the way. She was her own police force, finally turning herself in to the authorities. She understood when the time had come to end it all, whereupon she executed a brutal coincidence of panic and decision. She was no brooding Hamlet, whose tendency to read and re-read and to write down what he heard had granted him the temporal slack he needed to bring the whole house down. No doubt, Hamlet ends up sending himself the poisoned point by return mail and, like Emma, finally commits himself to a writing of suicide. But if they share the same poison, and even the banquets of the uneaten, one should not mix these up too readily, for *Madame Bovary* opens herself to an altogether different history of intelligibility, in fact, to another suicide pact, cosigned by a world that no longer limits its rotting to a singular locality of the unjust. This is not to say that Hamlet and his phantom have been dealt with definitively, but they have been left in suspension by an interrogating openness, a kind of ontological question or futural transmission running interference with the most serene channels of forgetfulness. Emma Bovary, she has been understood. And the material proliferation of critical works surrounding the novel does not refute this statement. On the contrary: No one has claimed to be puzzled by this enigma—she has been the clearing space, the translating machine through which an epoch renders itself intelligible, if not quite above itself.

§

Hamlet, De Quincey, Emma Bovary, Balzac, Baudelaire, William Burroughs, Artaud (and scores of others) urged upon us a thinking of human nourishment. If they were not quite vegetarians, they tried to nourish themselves without properly eating. Whether injecting themselves or smoking cigarettes or merely kissing someone, they rerouted the hunting grounds of the cannibalistic libido. In a certain manner of conscious monitoring, they refused to eat—and yet they were always only devouring, or drinking up the toxic spill of the Other. Drugs make us ask what it means to consume anything, anything at all. This is a philosophical question, to the extent that philosophy has always diagnosed health, that is, being-itself or the state of nonalienation, by means of its medico-ontological scanners.[21] Where does the experience of eating begin? What of the remains? Are drugs in some way linked to the management of remains? How has the body been drawn into the disposal systems of our technological age?

It is perhaps not surprising that every utterance linked to drugs has something to say about what is appropriable. In his introduction, William Burroughs writes, "The title means exactly what the words say: NAKED Lunch—a frozen moment when everyone sees what is on the end of every fork."[22] Prior to this frozen moment, Baudelaire, the first worthy reader of *Madame Bovary* according to Flaubert, remarked: "In order to digest natural as well as artificial happiness, it is first necessary to have the courage to swallow; and those who would most deserve happiness are precisely the ones upon whom cheerfulness, as conceived by mortals, has always had an emetic effect (*l'effet d'un vomitif*)."[23]

The possibility of an altogether other health, pointing as it does to the great vomiter, Nietzsche, has to do with the properly *improper* character of the body. We seem to be dealing with forces of inscription that relieve the body of itself while resisting its sublation into ideality, spirit, or consciousness. The *purification* of the body described by Baudelaire paradoxically maintains the body in its material, corruptible state of dis-integrity. As that which can swallow and throw up—naturally or artificially—the body rigorously engages the dynamics of becoming, surpassing itself without reducing itself to a passageway. These observations in fact model age-old concerns whose subscription to thought has been renewed by the way drugs negotiate the paracomestible substance.

§

Why should I begin my study of *Madame Bovary* in the mode of fiction? To fill a prescription; namely, that the provisions of the simulacrum be doubled. It is a method similar to the one I used three centuries ago for editing *The Sorrows of Young Werther.* There was another, more timely motive, which I did not discover until reading a passage from Gilles Deleuze in *Difference and Repetition:*

> On the one hand a book of philosophy ought to be a very particular kind of crime story, and on the other hand it should resemble science fiction. By crime story (*roman policier*) we mean that concepts should intervene, driven by a zone of presence, in order to resolve a local situation.[24]

This places our inquiry on the outer precincts of the detective genre, in the tradition of Sherlock Holmes, who was reputed, alas, to suffer from cocaine addiction.

PART THREE : EB ON ICE

It used to be that mediatic spaces were zoned outside of you. When you thought you felt like watching cable TV or listening to the radio, you would get up and switch the power on. This way you thought you were under a spell of spontaneity, internally combusted, and the external hallucinators would respond to your command. It was bizarre back then, everyone hoping they were autonomous, but in fact more or less hypnotized by these allotechnologies, held off at a distance that was just that much more fascinating. I thought about these things this morning when I went to get my implant packet, and the person ahead of me chose their six-month girloid program, which the doctor injected into her arm. She was already beginning to hear the music when she left, and she said it felt good. I needed a lot of silence mapped into my packet, because I had to cogitate. Still, right before I started writing I would need some stimulators, so I chose about sixteen sonic overlays. How did they do it in the old days, I wondered, relying on chance or inspiration, like waiting for winds to fill your sails? I picked the hologrammatology program, because I needed to be in several places at the same time, and

If the literature of electronic culture can be located in the works of Philip K. Dick or William Gibson, in the imaginings of a cyberpunk projection, or a reserve of virtual reality, then it is probable that electronic culture shares a crucial project with drug culture. This project should be understood in Jean-Luc Nancy's and Blanchot's sense of désoeuvrement—a project without an end or program, an unworking that nonetheless occurs, and whose contours we can begin to read.

I didn't want to fall into facile identifications. The activities of thinking were probably profoundly the same as before, but everything had changed. And yet, there had been a non-caesuric change. Nobody could scan the cut because we had experienced an interruption in history altogether different from the ones that had been prescribed.

Nietzsche was right when he predicted that the wasteland would grow. You, on the other hand, were asking for too much. There are no things that merge revelation and apocalypse—something you longingly called for. They just don't happen. Yes, of course. The ceaseless armageddon, the showdowns and steady threat of extinction, all these moves on a truth that cannot happen. You were unable to imagine a heterochronicity, a different break in history, non-apocalyptic—perhaps close to what used to be called a different Dispensation. If it happened more gradually, it didn't mean that things were less radical in their mutations. On the contrary. The contaminations and internalizations were harder to trace down; strange coalitions were forming, and the transvaluating machine was left running. What was considered desirable then, now seems weak, anachronistic. How could you have known the real frontiers?

It's not as if I was going to offer you therapeutic restitution in the future. You had to crash against your own mistakes. But you took too many people down with you. This was not going to be one of those narratorial spaces you get in the novel of *Bildung,* where, replaying *Wilhelm Meister,* I would be sitting up in the control tower, guiding you toward an ethical resolution. I was not in possession of your manuscript, and yet I knew what was going on. The political consequence of my position was to deny utopia, even as a *regulative* ideal. There was going to be no escape, no transcendence, no exteriority of the system we call political. No wonder you resisted me. I shouldn't have cut the cautionary protocols and theoretical rehearsals. You understood so very little about the chemical prosthesis which was the real, insubstantial vehicle constituting the virtual.

Sometimes I wonder why we revived you. Why do we turn to you in times of acute hestitation? As if you could beam forward the future of your own future by reassembling the past. You are a funny totem, you know, so full of sacred error.

It all goes back to the day when you activated the distinction between beings and things. You forgot one thing, though: immixation—dosages—and that's when you made your big mistake. You had the wherewithal to figure it out, the internal velocities and information flows. Even your systems of rendezvous carried the clue. All those electronic programs that depended upon discontinuous sequencings for their intelligibility. But you were too busy going after humanism's suspects, you had no time for a new inflection of being.

You were an ally of the great metaphysics, looking for epistemic breaks and clear cuts. All those border patrols along your unmodulated identities. It's odd that today we still worship you in a residual kind of way. Despite the calm, we need substitute mysticisms. You should have seen it coming. Especially when you housed electronic culture, which meant, as you said, a certain swipe at metaphysics. You got scared. Cybernetics was being superseded by the more sophisticated agents of artificial intelligence, but it had the lasting effect of retaining an essential distinction between human and machine. This is what you failed to see: that before all man-machinic hybridizations, a technology of the human was already in place. The age of the chemical prosthesis had already begun. Secretly, with phenomenal discretion.

I clicked into the interchronic project when it was learned that I could cogitate. When all epochality faded out, we started establishing communications with past dimensionalities. Sometimes we collided into futural flashes, because in the splays of heterochronicity, you couldn't linearize the aim the way they used to. I got promoted pretty fast and made transmissionary within a matter of three queus. This is why I'm talking to you now, resurrecting you, from a place you have not yet come to locate. Don't look for me in your unconscious or on your monitor, even less in that thing you still call a book. Your spaces are on my time now. That's why I need to seem less interested in the instrumentality or toolness of mediatic incursions than in the relation to a hallucinated exteriority that these reflect—or rather, in the place where the distinction between interiority and exteriority is radically suspended, and where this phantasmatic opposition is opened up. For these reasons I am less inclined to work the machine as an object than to observe the exscription of metaphysical cravings to which it calls attention.

• • •

After the explosion, there were only a few things left. The refrigerator apparently had been used as a strongbox. That's where I found these papers. They seemed to be very old, dating from the 1990s. I admit that what I saw in that refrigerator sickened me. The papers dealt with what was then called a "war on drugs." They were investigating a female subject, a certain Emma Bovary, who seemed to be a foreigner. Since Bovary was out of jurisdiction or from another era, they'd had a hard time proving she was dealing. Hence the doctor's report, the scenes at the detox clinic and the courtroom drama. In those days they didn't yet know that good drugs were always haunted or contaminated by bad drugs.[25]

Emma Bovary had busted a logic of reappropriation, collapsing the dreams of restoring a self. Drugs, a kind of circulating non-essence that originates in a foreign market or at home, hadn't been invented yet, but their concept was in place, in some place called Rouen. Not that that's where it all started—it had never not started. By the 1990s, however, they declared a war on "these artificial, pathogenetic, and foreign aggressions."[26] There was one document, supplied by a local authority, saying that the technology of drugs responded to the call of addiction. This document seemed unfinished, so I left it out. Someone else wrote that everything he had said about technology can be applied to drugs: acceleration, speed, inertia, the third interval.[27]

It seems that the ideals espoused by medicine and the addict were the same: to deaden the pain and separate from a poisonous maternal flux. Emma Bovary was apparently a grand self-medicator. Like others before her, she experienced the dangers of a belle âme: raptures that cut her off from reality, hallucinated plenitude and pure communication, a kind of hinge on transcendental telepathy. Everything she tried out—religion, reading, love rushes, getting dressed in the morning—had hallucinogenic, analgesic, stimulating, or euphorizing effects upon her. She would also experience tremendous crashes. The peak of drugs, as of love, was for her telepathy, a communication over distances. She demanded hallucinatory satisfaction of desire in a zone that no longer distinguished between need and desire. This Emma Bovary ran the paradoxical circuit of self-conservation. The circuit was installed with the discovery of God's insufficiency. Without the paternal metaphor holding things together, one was at a loss, one became the artisan of one's own body, fiddling around, experimenting, creating new parts or treating the psyche like an organ, a sick organ. One became a maniacal bricoleur of one's own body.[28] It wasn't clear then: was the body private property or not, could the authorities legislate zoning ordinances, or were pleasure and liberty values freely exercised upon a coded body? Shit was happening. God's fundamental breakdown, His out-of-serviceness and withdrawal from the scene, meant that she had to replace the emptiness with a symbolic authority. That's when the panic set in, the emergencies that invaded the entire scene. Nothing else mattered; she needed her dose, and she started responding like an addict to the alarm signals proliferating around her. She didn't care what she took. Hard or soft drugs were an opposition established by medical and legal institutions. The Other was devastated, without address. Who were you going to call upon or appeal to? She would have to mime another plenitude. She started elaborating this Other as absence, and began her work of producing secrets. Alternately proud and anguished, above all secretive, she learned that the formation of secrecy engages a relation to absence and separation; she was working over the etymology of the signifier, trying to recover the substance that was separated from her. She started working overtime, making an orifice operate its relation to emptiness and to time. It was like a narcissistic overinvestment of an organ, but an organ that wasn't merely an organ. Like Glover had said, any substance can function like a drug.[29] One thing was sure: the addict was working what was wanting, missing, hurting. Freud had once claimed, in *Civilization and Its Discontents,* that pain is imperious, obeying only the action of the toxin that suppresses it.

It seems pretty clear from these papers that Emma Bovary never did any real work. Failing to make any responsible effort, she also failed to meet the requirements of an authentic alterity. She was more into forgetting and the simulacrum than truth. This would never be forgiven. It didn't matter whether what she did was comestible, smokable or shootable; she was a hallucinator, a creature par excellence of the simulacrum.

Emma Bovary was executed by a disastrous economy of painkillers. Her fictions quickly turned into devouring creditors. They were submitted to an intensified law of supply and demand, the *suppléance* of an addict's knowing body. It is a knowing related to unknowing. The massive distress signals from beyond any pleasure principle.

But what were these papers doing in a refrigerator in Alameda County? It must have had to do with the fact that America was taking suicide pills in those days, spreading the Jonestown effect on a rebound from exile. America still had to take drugs seriously, to stop *using* them for brute and primitive ends. The right wing's dependency on drugs was well known. No one knew how to disrupt the power of legal prescriptions that continued unthinkingly to make claims about substance abuse and the metaphysical subject. There were some commandos of residual resistance. They were wondering where thinking could take place so it would be dispensed to the poor, the body-broken, the racially hallucinated other? They figured drugs, this non-essence, had to be submitted to thought and not merely legislated out of the political body—and what a body it was!—plugging orifices, building muscle. Still, I don't know what Emma Bovary was doing in that refrigerator. It should have been a more direct hit, like Burroughs, Artaud, Michaux, or maybe something from the American drunkyards, like Poe, Faulkner, London, Chandler, Hammet, and the others. As I read the documents I realized that she was the body on which these urges started showing, almost naturally, prior to the time the technological prosthesis became available on the streets and drugs had become an effect of institution, convention, law. She hit the streets, too, roaming around, breaking out in cold sweats, hiding under veils. The whole addiction thing was a kind of veil, covering over and enshrouding her face, drained and sallow. She was under pressure to preserve a body, but this meant destroying her own body. *"Her own body"*—what a joke! All sorts of forces inscribed this body like so much invisible graffiti. She declared war on the real, this unknown horror, she put out the call for a drug culture. She worked out of her own abysses, hunting down the imaginary phallic supplement.

It took me quite a while to decide on publishing these papers. I haven't shown them to anyone, in part because I didn't particularly want to be associated with this discovery. Despite everything, Emma Bovary had had a pure body, she belonged to an unpolluted era of literature. Of course, this was a phantasm. No one really believed it. But still, they wanted to keep it clean. They were straight.

The horizon of drugs is the same as that of literature: they share the same line, depending on similar technologies and sometimes suffering analogous crackdowns before the law. They shoot up fictions, disjuncting a whole regime of consciousness. Someone once said that literature, as a modern phenomenon dating from the sixteenth or seventeenth century, was contemporaneous with European drug addiction. When I saw that refrigerator, I knew there was going to be trouble. I had gone through a lot myself, recently. Problems with eating or sleeping, and then this house was blown apart. I took the papers and started reading them that night. A sympathy developed for Emma Bovary and even her investigators. I couldn't stop reading, it was like I was becoming these persons. All forms of identification that are structuring emerge from a trauma, or from a reserve of what is missing. I knew that much. So now I want to go public with these papers. I'm not exactly sure why, maybe because back then, someone started thinking about drugs before the place blew up.

I hope you don't mind going through this again. It won't be easy. I ask the telereader to become a friend to Madame Bovary, to spend the night with her. It was another, agonizing night of withdrawal.

PART FOUR : SHAME

"Emma, intoxicated with sadness"

"Instead of poison shame was necessary." This critical judgment was delivered by the chief prosecutor on the occasion of *Madame Bovary*'s indictment. A compression of ethical phrasing, it emerges in the shadow of the law, where moral and political evaluations crowd the dénouement of Gustave Flaubert's "realist" novel. But the literary fact remains that Madame Bovary swallowed poison, not her pride.

“Léon hesitated, as
though struggling against
the pharmacist’s spell.”

Our narcotic modernity.

“As for the rest of the world, it was lost to her; it had no specific location and scarcely seemed to exist at all.”

"Instead of poison shame was necessary." It's not that Emma Bovary resisted the path of sacrifice. She kept her anguish a secret, commiting an interiorizing violence. Her violence was, however, on the "bad" side of interiority, in a nonmoral sense. The poison was still too material for the court, too proudly inflected by a certain individualism. Shame, at least, would have bound her to the community, within sight of a collective creditor.

"Did not love, like Indian plants, require prepared soil and special temperatures?"

"Instead of poison shame was necessary." In a novel whose rhythm is governed by swallowing attacks, maternal rage constitutes the first substance to be assimilated. Of the primordial Madame Bovary, mother of Charles, it is asserted:

Then her pride rebelled; she withdrew into herself, swallowing her rage with a mute stoicism which she maintained until her death.[30]

The novel is about swallowing maternal rage.

PART FIVE : SCORING LITERATURE

I

And then there is the other side of *Madame Bovary*, billowing out, discreetly creased, cut to the body like her extravagant wardrobe: there is the side, or the edge, rather, of institutional inscription. Flaubert handed her over to the authorities at a relatively early stage; in fact, he had forced her entry into an encyclopedia of institutional determinations. In a way, she would never have a 'natural' body. It was refracted, cut up, in one of those multiply hinged mirrors. When she stepped up to look at herself, the glare of medical, legal, religious, and marital institutions made it hard to discern the reflection of a pure contour of self. Interiorizing the sense of blur, zoning out, Madame Bovary felt weak that day, and thought she should see the priest.

II

Instead, she took another hit. Meanwhile, there was the obstinate grimace of the pharmacy next door. When you looked at it up close, you could still read the ever prescriptive language of Monsieur Homais, the apothecary. She dissolves in the novel; he, on the contrary—he hardens into a position. If Homais has the last word, it is because pharmacy is the mastery of drugs.

III

Flaubertian leaks

The writing of secretion

In many ways, *Madame Bovary* is a novel about suicidal anguish, about exploring the limits of interiorizing violence. The motivation to suicide never simply involves the extinction of one person, but tends to arrive from another agency. It hits you with the violence of a non-address. Innocent bystander at the event of your suicide, you sometimes miss, that is, you have made an attempt. But this time you did not miss the Other. This means: at the extreme limits of experience, the gesture offers a lever for killing something or someone, the Persecutor. The death rush disposes—sometimes—of the harassing other, eliminating him. You succeed in secreting the other. At the place where existence and finitude touch, the harassed one threatens to take someone down with him, producing an ultimatum, and sometimes you win.

Madame Bovary committed total suicide; her nullity affirms itself and it is not immediately clear who or what she took with her. Her death establishes no discernible order of being for or beyond herself. On the contrary, a certain narcosis spreads its effects through the body of the text, numbing its articulations. The future is dulled. This has little to do with the suicidal grandeur of Empedocles, nor even with the tender desperation of young Werther. Instead, a certain economy has been exhausted . . . she goes broke. She has passed at the level of low energy rather than from a revealed side of destructive *jouissance*. The aftereffects of her suicide are no less dim. Her husband locks himself into mourning and breaks with a more original Madame Bovary, his mother. (In fact, there were two Madame Bovarys prior to Emma, who starts on the edge of degenerescence.) Her brutalized child, Berthe, suffers a fading, sacrificed by Flaubert at the novel's end to a series of humiliations. (He leaves little doubt about it, Emma Bovary was a child abuser.) Her father, devastated, leaves; her lovers endure remote and pitiless lives. The poison-giver, Justin, experiences hysterical grief. And so, Emma's phallic body has passed out of circulation, vacating the premises.

In short, it seems that nothing much happens that would surrender a sign or a revealing from Emma Bovary's death. No one figure turns up to explain the cause for her murderous rage. Her face does not slip into the attendant folds of a predecessor, as does Werther's when his bleeding head breaks apart over *Emilia Galotti;* there is no transcendental inflection to transport her elsewhere, no signal of a genealogical circuitry. She does not manage to eliminate any particular force or figure, though it is said that ink flows from her mouth. In this nothingness that menaces death with a loss of symbology, two discrete events take place, however. Flaubert has attacks of nausea and throws up while committing Emma Bovary to suicide. And, in the novel, the apothecary, Homais, survives to receive a national prize. This survival signals the commencement of the pharmaceutical wars.

IV

If the novel goes on after the death of Madame Bovary, drawn out by Homais, it is in order to territorialize another kind of drug story. The same store from which Emma drew the suicidal poison returns to occupy the scene at the end of the novel. In the wake of a great nothingness, the pharmacy is figured to exceed the commerce of hell: "il fait une clientèle d'enfer" (366) ("Mr. Homais now has more patients than the devil himself could handle" [302]). The erection of this institution (over Emma's dead body) calls attention to itself, and not only because it is shown to be the institution of institutions, the storehouse of prescriptive language and pseudoscientific writing. It acquires legal sanctity from a structure at once fragile and constant, a mix of fable and belief. Thus, of its guardian, the *homme* and homeopath, we learn: "l'autorité le ménage et l'opinion publique le protège" (366)("the authorities treat him with deference and public opinion supports him" [303]). Following the uncontrolled patterns of ingestion which had organized Emma Bovary's losing economy, a condensation and restoration occur: every medical dispensary holds in reserve a store of poison. In a sense, Flaubert's novel breaks the ground for a modern drug store chain. Beyond evil, the drug store is a signifying chain that leaves even the devil in the dust.

The building site has had to be situated beyond good and evil because in the novel negotiations with the discourse adjudicating such matters have collapsed. Two attendants have watched over Emma's body. Of the two, one constellates a customary but unreflected leftover, something that Emma herself had discarded. Representatives of religion and the drug store keep watch over her, squabble, snore loudly and eat. In a moment of extreme agitation, Emma Bovary had sought the religious pill. It offered nothing, revealing neither painkilling qualities nor even those vague consolations of the mild tranquilizer. The drug store was still open.

Despite the grim irony with which Flaubert sets up Homais for life, something very serious occurs by means of an underground thematics that has led to the consolidation of a drug store monopoly. For the drug store in *Madame Bovary* guarantees the preservation of a cadaverous presence while marking the place of its otherness to itself. The drug store figures a legalized reproach to uncontrolled or street drugs but at the same time argues for the necessity of a certain drug culture. Indeed, the critical question that Flaubert poses through the novel concerns the possibility of culture divested of hallucinogens. There is no culture without a drug culture, even if this is to be sublimated to pharmaceuticals.

V

At a time when the concept itself of politics is dissolving into a unanimous war against drugs, Flaubert urges upon us a reading of the untimely, that is, of the phantasms and phantoms that invest the institution of a drug store.

VI

The narrative allegorizes the split over drug control and a condemnation of street drugs at a number of corners that organize the textual cartography: "'Drunkenness ought to be dealt with more severely!' said the apothecary" (132). The injunction comes around the bend, crashing through the text, driven as it is by an unruly coachman. The scene of the uncontrolled coach, a sort of public *bateau ivre,* presents the complementary "other" to the drive of amorous pursuit, a scene that Flaubert had to defend in court. The drunken coach and the love coach belong to the same public company, though only the latter received a court citation. The scene is unforgettable, finally, because its taking place dodges representation. Circulating openly, it never arrives at telling. It drives the open wound of secrecy to another place, to a kind of public unconscious.

Perhaps you were there on that hot summer day when the lovers were locked into the closure of absolute embrace, a cab that was impermeable to narration. Suddenly the window opened like a gaping mouth, ejecting a shredded text. The wind started scattering the remains of a letter of rupture that Emma had written to Léon. We felt we could tell what was happening, sitting at the square with our panachés. The thing kept coming around, as our companion observed, "a carriage with drawn blinds which kept appearing and reappearing, closed as tightly as a tomb and rocking like a ship" (211). He later confided that the coach staged a paradigm of interlocking private and public textual maneuvering. The most private of acts was to be performed in a public space from which it nevertheless concealed itself, evoking something as openly private, the open space of a sealed casket. (We shall see how Madame Bovary's public display of internal violence is aligned with a similar structure of intoxication.) The coach is a supplier of essential metaphor; poised in the market place, at once open and closed, like a posted letter, it conveys the crucial link between the open market and clandestine traffic. It circumscribes the space within which drug traffic issues a problematics of 'public health.' At this point, however, we have left the apothecary hanging the drunk. His faculty for judgment was aroused by the disjunctive movements of a carriage: "The coachman, who was drunk, suddenly dozed off, and in the distance the mass of his body could be seen above the hood, between the two lanterns, swaying back and forth with the pitching of the thorough braces" (132).

The apothecary, whose calling depends almost entirely upon a stock market of public opinion, would like to see a bulletin board put up on the door of the town hall "for the special purpose of posting a list of the names of everyone who's been intoxicated by alcohol during the week. It would be useful from a statistical point of view, too, because it would constitute a public record that could"—we in fact never learn what this record could do, for its promise dissolves into ellipses. Still, this may constitute the first declaration of war on unregulated drugs, passing from an apothecary's mouth to a public denunciation of guilty parties. The public record would keep tabs on the deconstituting body.

The drunk, like the adulterous Emma, liberates uncontrolled signs into a public sphere. Their display irradiates a mimetic poisoning which, once absorbed, would set off an entire population of innocent bystanders in the same movement of dissolution. Like the work which contains them, they become killer texts, triggering a chain reaction of uncontained mimetic caliber. Thus even translators of such a text are endangered by the effects of contagion.*

* Eleanor Marx Aveling, the daughter of Karl Marx, one of the early translators of *Madame Bovary* into English, committed suicide in much the same manner as Emma.

They—the adulterers of morals—stage for the socius an irremediable destructive satisfaction; in other words, they stage the literality of the satisfaction derived from auto-destruction. The automobility of this small cartel is what interests us here.

If the scenes of drunkenness and adulterous trespass are constantly put into communication with one another, this is in the first place because Flaubert seems to register gradations of the word "adultery" according to the distillation of its etymology. Adultery means that which alters the mind, falsifying and modifying its natural inflection. In its concept adultery is indissociable from what today we call mind-altering drugs: "Adultery comes from a Latin verb that signifies *alter,* and nothing in fact more alters things and feelings."[31] The mind-altering project casts about for a premise of which it can presume an original purity of mind, a non-contaminated naturalness that would be in harmony with convention and lawful conduct (the surprising intersection of nature and law would put a stop sign before those conducted by a smashed driver, for instance). That which has avoided the zone of experience marked by *adultery* fits simultaneously in the groove of the natural as it inscribes the institution. Out of this tension of doubling and loosening the stakes of adultery, Flaubert concocts an entire ethos of drug culture avant la lettre. A seamless collapse of drugs into crime, of *adultery* into outlaw, is something that his probing sensibility would not hazard. Still, he was always up against the law.

VII

It is still necessary to demonstrate the structure of addiction that governs Emma's conduct in the novel, the drug wars which she originates and which range from her dependence on chemical prostheses, as in the case of make-up, to the intoxication which she imperiously seeks. The "objects" of her intoxication consist of non-containable substances whose traces we still have to analyze. While the drug store, as social investment, is on the side of truth (science, remedy, statistics), Emma is a subject of the simulacrum. However, both are linked to a reading of non-essence which is at the base of the valuation wars raging in the textual body.

VIII

As subject of the simulacrum, Emma Bovary becomes an addict at a young age. Her mind, oblique corridor of private screenings, was always already altering.[32] Perhaps it would be of some usefulness, before tracking her history, to set up a parallel tape which reads off the imaging of adultery to which Flaubert was rooted. In *Les Français peints par eux-mêmes* (1841), the essay "La Femme adultère" warns: "Once started down this tortuous path, a woman cannot stop herself."[33] A more recent treatment of the phenomenon, from within the American university, argues that adulterous transgression is something that "drags the heroine out of existence."[34] The article pinpoints the source of trespass to reading and daydreaming, operations dominated by fantasy. The errant wife is in fact "stepping out of bounds when she secretly indulges in the reading of scandalous novels and in daydreaming identification with women who slink about the never-neverland of wish-fulfillment. This peculiar susceptibility to the printed word is perhaps more generally assumed to be an attribute of woman, rather than just adultress: throughout the Romantic era, a woman is one who reads novels as a substitute for active living; she regresses into moral and legal minority the moment she marries. I hardly need point out that *Madame Bovary* is a fiction about the danger of fictions."[35] Despite the symptomatic tendencies to which generalities are susceptible, these observations in fact par-

psychotrope

ticipate in the novel's coherency. Strictly speaking, then, the adultress does not disappoint institutional expectations simply by sleeping out but also by setting off a certain libidinal faculty that can, at the extreme limit, remain objectless. The "woman" regulates her dosage of fantasy, secretly indulging in the fiction of identification with a community of non-substantial others. Indeed, the adultress destabilizes the conventional bounds of the legitimate object by viewing with in-difference the substance of the other man. Structures of repetition and substitution take precedence over the "real" qualities of the other. A question of transference, in short, that perturbs the order of things. When you are "intoxicated with love," shot up with fictions and heavily transferring, who is this Other, does he have an essence?

Emma Bovary will fold her objects into a serial indifference which always underscores the addictive profile of her acts. She figures as the figure invested in something other than "active living," escaping mythemes of heroic as well as quotidian being around which, historically, virility has been organized: phallogocentrism. According to the logic of the above cited argument, it is not woman in her designation as adultress that poses the principal menace; it is the figuration of woman and the attendant political effects that perturb the economy of being. "A woman" is the mark of a fissure in active living, a thing of the sidelines, beside the point and attracted *actively* to a substitute for active living. (This shows what a symptom woman continues to be, one in touch with vampiric death threats, for what else can a substitute for "active living" evoke?) She takes another way, a way, we could say, of pathivity. Passive but on the way, she exposes herself to a sort of foreign aggression (so much is foreign to this woman: everything "active" belongs to a foreign currency . . .). Inactive living is another way of saying active destruction—a woman finds a substitute. In this case, she consumes novels. The solitary experiment of eluding a politics of community (by choice or by imposition) frees her into a domain of precarious pleasure, as it detaches her from active or responsible living. On the side of the letter, wearing shades to shield her from the blazing living logos, she is a reader of epitaphs, in exile from living reality.

What do we hold against the drug addict?
What do we hold against the drug addict?
What do we hold against the drug addict?

. . . that he cuts himself off from the world, in exile from reality, far from objective reality and the real life of the city and the community; that he escapes into a world of simulacrum and fiction. We disapprove of hallucinations. . . . We cannot abide the fact that his is a pleasure taken in an experience without truth.[36]

Pleasure and play, Derrida explains, are not in themselves condemned unless they are inauthentic and devoid of truth.[37] This opens the political question of literary fiction and a certain feminine vulnerability before its seduction and charm. Literature is said to cast its spell over the feminized reader; she cannot stop reading, she is captivated by this other that opens itself up to her. She finds herself seduced by a hallucination; nothing is properly hidden behind hallucination. Confirming non-mimetic values, the asserted clarity of the hallucinatory spell uncovers an order of being that has little to do with truth-value. The seduction recommences every day, on every page. It is a politics of non-satiation. Wholly absorbed by this other which she absorbs, she sits in her corner or sometimes goes out on the streets for more. The addict, like this woman, wants more. Reinscribing the way in which the creature of the simulacrum finds himself driven from the community (by Plato, etc.), Flaubert diverts the argument toward the feminine prosthesis.

IX

The structure of addiction, and even of drug addiction in particular, is anterior to any empirical availability of crack, ice or street stuff. This structure and necessity are what Flaubert discovers and exposes. A quiver in the history of madness (to which no prescription of reason can be simply and rigorously opposed), the chemical prosthesis, the mushroom or plant, respond to a fundamental structure, and not the other way around. Of course, one can be hooked following initiation and exposure but even this supposes a prior disposition to admitting the injectable phallus.

A mysticism in the absence of God, a mystical transport going nowhere, like the encapsulated carriage once again. This is not far from Bataille's "inner experience" of ecstasy, a "mysticisme dégagé de ses antécédents religieux . . ." that is, a mysticism without mysticism or experience without truth.[38]

What do we hold against the drug addict?

What do we hold against the drug addict?

It is possibly of some importance that a flower of a different sort, a hallucinated woman, be made to experiment with what we can still call the transcendental street drug—or with feminine incorporations of a phallic flux. A strong concept of purity shot through with virility will come to dominate the history of Madame Bovary, who bears so many traces of manliness.

Any way you look at it, Emma Bovary carries the marks

"a pince-nez which she carried, like a man, tucked in between two buttons of her bodice"

of her many incorporations of a foreign body. We have yet to grasp the male sex she carries with her, for Emma is not a simply gendered woman. Her prime injections of a foreign body follow the multiple lines of an interiorizing violence.

X

What do we hold against the drug addict?

In the first place, Emma's moments of libidinal encounter are frequently described as experiences of intoxication. The second place, however, may be of more interest. In the second place, then, we discover that drugs, when submitted to Flaubert's precision of irony, are after all not viewed as a conduit of escape but as present at the base of life:

An evening with her husband, Charles Bovary. How could she get rid of him?

> **He seemed to her contemptible, weak and insignificant. How could she get rid of him? What an endless evening! She felt numb, as though she had been overcome by opium fumes. (217)**

Emma judges Charles to be a weak man. The judgment is sounded from a position of feminine virility. His nullity, overwhelming, turns her into a hit man (how to get rid of him?). From the sense of the deadening infinitude of this confrontation, the threatening limitlessness of what is mediocre, Emma reconstitutes existence as an effect of an overdrawn downer. Not only does this passage argue for the refinement of difference—this opiate acts differently from other insinuations of her substance/husband abuse—it also shows the opium base to be at the bottom of life. Life in its essential normalcy (they are at the dinner table when she ODs) yields to death because it is on the side of an endlessness that numbs. And so Emma Bovary's body gets rigid with the presentiment of nothingness.

Like the Western world, there is no place or moment in the life of Madame Bovary that could be designated as genuinely clean or drug-free, because being exposed to existence, and placing one's body in the grips of a temporality that pains, produces a rapport to being that is addictive, artificial and beside itself. The history of mood, or aesthetic theory, from Baumgarten to Heidegger deals ecstasy (Nietzsche: *Rausch*), zoning out (Schopenhauer), inspired trance (Kant). But Emma, she is only a rookie trafficking in abstract forms of forgetting. She suffers endlessly from her finitude, sitting there face to face with her husband. "She felt numb," which is to say, she felt non-feeling. Life assigns itself to her with a drained sensation of its own nothingness.[39] If Emma is going to take drugs seriously, it will be only in order to diminish the power, to decrease the dosage that numbs. She needs a counter-drug, something to repel the ruthless continuity of the opiate, "life." In another sense, this need inscribes the same kind of logic that consists in taking drugs for the sake of an experience, that is: "for the experience" of that which hounds the limits of experience but nonetheless belongs to a decisive zone of experience.

Life's vacant terror

To the extent that drugs delineate the experience of experience as a moment which slips or turns away from responsible consciousness and self-stability, they offer a reflection of the non-present nature of experience whose marked interpretability follows lines of delay and reconstitution, forgetting and *Nachträglichkeit*.

What then is the difference between these experiential zones? It's too soon to tell, and one doesn't want to fall into the pits of defending Being-as-drugs (of the ecstatic or calming sort). Still, it is absolutely necessary to hazard a preliminary hypothesis and to take risks. What is Emma, literary philtre, on to? On the one hand, drugs are linked to a mode of departing, to desocialization—much like the activity of writing, to the extent that it exists without the assurance of arriving anywhere. Considered non-productive and somehow irresponsible, a compulsive player of destruction, Being-on-drugs resists the production of value which, on another, more Bataillean register, indicates that it disrupts the production of meaning. Emma exists somewhere between the drug addict and the writer (she is a writer; at least she owns the equipment, the stylus).[40] Obsessed and entranced, narcissistic, private, unable to achieve transference, the writer often resembles the addict. This is why every serious war on drugs comes from a community that is at some level of consciousness also hostile to the genuine writer, the figure of drifter/dissident, which it threatens to expel. Like the addict, such a writer is incapable of producing real value or stabilizing the truth of a real world. The differences between them are not difficult to discern, and yet a single logic of parasitism binds the two activities to each other. The drug addict offers her body to the production of hallucination, vision or trance, a production assembled in the violence of non-address. This form of internal saturation of self, unhooked from a grander effective circuit, marks the constitutive adestination of the addict's address. Going nowhere fast, as we say, Madame Bovary in this regard signs up for the drug program to the extent that she resumes the violence of non-address.

> **She had bought herself a blotter [*un buvard*], writing-case, pen-holder, and envelopes although *she had no one to write to*. . . . (52) (italics added)**[41]

With nowhere to go and little to do, these missives, along with the equipment that maintains them, can only be routed inwardly. But it is an inwardness of diminished interiority, a kind of dead letter box—an impasse in destination. Still, writing for no one to no address counts for something; it is the writer's common lot. For Flaubert, this movement of the simulacrum without address (or in another idiom: without purpose, point) is associated with the toxic pleasure of a certain narcissism:

> **I have condemned myself to write for myself alone, for my own personal amusement, the way one smokes or rides.[42]**

It is important to weigh this violence of non-address because it designates a most vulnerable type of writing that is, like smoking, susceptible to acts of nihilism, burning out. Unaddressed or unchanneled pleasure, condemnation to solitary confinement, with or without a community of smokers, belongs to the registers of a "feminine" writing in the sense that it is neither phallically aimed nor referentially anchored, but scattered like cinders. At no point a prescriptive language or pharmacological ordinance, it is rather a writing on the loose, running around without a proper route, even dispensing with the formalities of signing. The impropriety of such writing—which returns only to haunt itself, refusing to bond with community or affirm its health and value—consistently reflects a situation of depropriation, a loss of the proper. Thus the heroine (who is also, sometimes, Flaubert: "Madame Bovary, c'est moi!") not only has no one to write to, but also lacks a proper name ("'Madame Bovary! Everyone calls you that! And it's not even your name—it's someone else's . . . someone else's!' He buried his face in his hands" [134].) Still, this is the name that entitles the book, and cosigns its cover. But the countersignatory functions like a bad check, destined to collapse upon itself and bounce. The destinee of a drug addict or such a writer responds to the hallucinated other of Kafka's *Judgment,* the "friend in Russia" whose existence a paternally musculated law can at any time deny or appropriate. But even when the other is smoked out, there's a chance that writing will take place.

XI

Someone has referred to *Madame Bovary* as a paranoiac text. It wasn't me.[43] Constantly on the lookout for details, it feels entrapped by a closurally threatening movement of the real; additionally, it makes certain obsessional pacts with itself, not letting very much slip by its screening devices. It has the clandestine rapport to machinery for which paranoid strategists are famous. Surveillance apparatuses, the listening device, and the magnifying glass all belong to its narratology. Flaubert himself developed a rhetoric of machinery to describe his activity of writing. Not quite at the level of Dr. Schreber's *Memoirs,* the narrative gestures are nevertheless too surgical to evade nervous technicity.

On the narrative level of textual experience, the eruption of paranoia is felt at those times when Emma Bovary gets a hit. When signs are everywhere readable, signification becomes persecutory. Take one morning when "she glanced around uneasily, looking intently at every figure moving on the horizon, at every dormer window in the village from which she might be seen. She listened for the sound of footsteps, voices and plows, and whenever she heard something she would stop in her tracks, paler and more trembling than the leaves of the poplars swaying above her head.

One morning as she was coming back she suddenly thought she saw a long rifle being aimed at her." (142–43)

"and her soul, sinking into that intoxication"

Such passages of sensitive terror dominate the residue of intoxication. And so the narrative, as codependent and accomplice, shows Emma adopting strategies to help her avoid coming down from what it calls "love." "Love had intoxicated (*enivrée*) her at first, and she had thought of nothing beyond it. But now that it had become an essential part of her life she was afraid she might lose part of it, or even that something might arise to interfere with it" (142). On the loose and on the run, she dives into a paranoid crash position which organizes her "downfall" in the novel.

XII

GOING DOWN

What goes hand in hand with her decline is a kind of crash economy, an exorbitant expenditure with no reserve: we call this "narcodollars." Quite understandably, little has been said about Emma Bovary's radically losing economy, save to mention perhaps her creditor, a certain Mr. High and Happy—Monsieur Lheureux. No doubt this topos fails to gain easy currency within readings that limit themselves to variants of housewifely neurosis, unmastered lovesickness, "Bovarysme," or even frustrated writing habits. Yet all these conditions are linked to expenditure. To support her habit—while to a certain degree objectless, it is still maintained as a substance in the novel—Emma Bovary invests a field of liquidity that involves incredible manipulation of interest rates, capital gains, mortgaging and even, indeed, laundered money. She keeps a whole village economy vibrating, cutting deals like a shrewd cartel. She is dealing however for her own consumption and not trading properly. She borrows too much (in the way she borrows—cites, lives off—literature). At any rate, Lheureux pulls a fast one and the narcodollars overwhelm her. In the end, she's liquidated.

liquidare (*med.*)

The momentum of a savage cash flow cannot be contained by a reading of *Madame Bovary* that restricts itself merely to following her down the adulterous path, how-

Why do these toxic eruptions transfix a woman's body? Why could it not have been Monsieur Bovary *that inaugurated a certain form of quotidian psychosis? Perhaps you find these questions unsatisfying. The response, even more so: it all comes from the issue of her body, the sudden spill of liquid, the way she's stained and shredded by anguish. Coming from her, originating in her, it is nonetheless a foreign body, ever replacing the newly born body. Catastrophe of the liquid oozing. She has a mortgage out on her body, a monthly payment.*

Freud: "I am beginning only now to understand the neurosis of anguish; menstruation is its physiological prototype, constituting a toxic condition which has as its basis an organic process." (Letter to Fliess, 1 March 1896) ever charming this might seem. There's the question of a libidinal economy, of course, and of the spermatic economy in which she spends herself. Her lovers, fairly well endowed with capital flow, do not leave clues as to why she should be running such a relentlessly losing economy. Her uncontrollable expenditure at once points to a complete divestiture of property (she secretly sells the inheritance and property of her husband) and to the flow that is being drawn from her. She quite literally is being drained of resources: something is vampirizing Emma Bovary. Now this drainage which in itself produces nothing—there is no transfer of energy or funds—will terminate only when the cash flow gushes out of her mouth at the scene of her suicide. This is when the concept itself of currency becomes assimilated to her circulatory systems. Within the larger economy of the novel, these speculations are nothing new, for the narrative has dropped hints along the way.

liquidare (*med.*)

When we first came upon her, Emma Bovary, displaying symptoms of auto-vampirism, was running an internally regulated circulation, a currency whose losses she could initially absorb:

> **as she sewed, she kept pricking her fingers and raising them to her lips to suck them. (12)**

Suturing and opening, stitching and wounding—she at once textures and bleeds. Into her mouth. The marks of a vampire should in any case come as no surprise to anyone familiar with Charles's taste in women, for his first wife—the second Madame Bovary—"was skinny; she had long teeth" (16). When, on the other hand, Emma's vampiric traits arise, they are accompanied by another trademark of a foreign body invasion, which is to say, she begins to exhibit virile features, she enters a semiosis of masculine properties: "She had a shell-rimmed pince-nez which she carried, like a man, tucked in between two buttons of her bodice" (13). Or, again:

> **Finally even those who still had doubts lost them when she was seen stepping out of the Hirondelle one day wearing a tight, mannish-looking vest . . . (165)**

Periodically growing signs of an indwelling alterity, Emma Bovary appears to suffer incorporation. There is something other gnawing at her, a beloved, but at the same time a Persecutor whom she has to feed and nourish. This may in part furnish an explanation for her inability to
nurture
her
child.

XIII

Crack Baby

Of the scandals that the novel provoked, one concerned precisely her brutalization of Baby. The budget cuts that she initiates belong elsewhere; money is associated with futurity in general but with her daughter's *Bildung* in particular. This is no sentimental education. Refusing to save money, Emma ruins the future and equally refuses to save her daughter, Berthe. There will be no growth, no development. Absolute bankruptcy. At the end, diminished and irrecuperably down on her luck, Berthe, ruined by her mother, more or less indentures herself to a distant relative, encountering the virtual dead end of a humiliated afterlife. ("An aunt took charge of the child's upbringing. She is poor and has put her to work in a cotton mill to earn her living" [302].)

But Emma was from the first a child-abuser, and this leads us to wonder what's eating her. Manifestly developing a structure of dependency, she cannot herself sustain a dependent. It is rather clearly stated that she cannot admit another woman into her life. Seeing her child for the first time, she faints, abandons it to a wet nurse and finally, supported by her suitor, Léon, visits it and quickly becomes disgusted. The child throws up on the mother who will keep it down until the end.

The nausea of motherhood.

The scene of this disgust, shared by mother and daughter, has skirted a cemetery.

> **To reach the wet-nurse's house they had to run left at the end of the street, as though going to the cemetery. (79)**

One could see, runs the description, "a pig on a manure pile, or cows wearing breast harnesses . . . while in front of them a swarm of flies buzzed in the warm air" (79). These passages, setting up the maternal demand, constitute the place to which we shall have to return. Incessantly. The house in which she had stowed away her child, marking an utter inversion of the Mosaic myth, is set where

> **A stream of dirty water was trickling over the grass, and all around were a number of nondescript rags, knitted stockings, a short red calico wrapper and a large, thick sheet spread out on the hedge. At the sound of the gate the wet-nurse appeared, carrying with one arm a child that was sucking her breast. With her other hand she was pulling a poor sickly little boy whose face was covered with scrofula sores. He was the son of a Rouen knit-goods dealer; too busy with their shop to take care of him, his parents had boarded him out in the country. . . . a Mathieu Laensberg almanac lay on the dusty mantelpiece among gun flints, candle ends and pieces of tinder. The clutter in the room was completed by a picture of Fame blowing her trumpet; it had no doubt been cut out of some perfume advertisement and was now fastened to the wall with six shoe nails. . . . standing in the midst of such squalor . . . Madame Bovary blushed; turned away, fearing there might have been a certain impertinence in his**

It had just thrown up on her collar.

But Madame Bovary was not too busy to take care of her child.

eyes. Then she put the baby back in its cradle: it had just thrown up on her collar. The wet-nurse quickly wiped it off, assuring her it wouldn't show. (80)

Destructed landscape. Libidinal rescue attempts. Blush. Disgust. Madame Bovary is freaked. We—we have to stick to this scene, if only because it returns. The communication of nausea from mother to daughter is unremitting. Where does the circuit commence? In the first place, the cemetery. No, let us keep this for the last place. Grazing the cemetery, Flaubert unfolds a scene of natural bodies, all somehow ironized and polluted by the dirty stream—the nurturing cow, harnessed, the mother body of the wet-nurse. In this landscape of dreary but resolute naturalness, Emma stands out like an artifice, an obstinate resistance to the organic. And this is something to keep in mind: her refusal of the organic body, her startling capacity for disgust and toxicity, gradually grow into the figuration par excellence of the addicted subject. What do we hold against the addict?

In the name of this organic and originary naturalness of the body we declare and wage war on drugs.[44]

In the work containing Madame Bovary, the only originary naturalness is drawn from the body of a cow. But in order to evoke naturality, it bears the marks of equipment and artifice; the moment the animal body enters literature, it, too, belongs to technicity and artifice. Natural bodies are those of the cows, and horses,* that travel the text. The

*This is why Rodolphe seduces Emma at an animal fair, against which she stands out but into which he ineluctably draws her. But she is not simply a human animal in the zoomorphic mapping that Flaubert has prepared.

nature of the human is shown to be on the edge of decay and dilapidation, whereas everything that is staked on beauty is on the side of artifice or the somehow foreign (this can be Paris). The tensions rumbling through the novel derive from a secret war against artificial, pathogenetic and foreign invasions. And thus Emma Bovary invades the space of the infant as a missile of toxicity, an emetic mother, artificial and dangerous. Invading and polluting what is naturally polluted ("dirty water"), she inspires toxic desire in others. As she is about to leave, the wet-nurse thus asks Emma Bovary for coffee and alcohol.

> **"if you'd just let me have"—she gave her a supplicating look—"a little jug of brandy," she said at last. (81)**

She is dealing, even over the body of her child.

> **"I'll rub your little girl's feet with it; they're as tender as your tongue." (81)**

Tenderness

Emma, in any case, cannot feed her child, she cannot bend her body to postures of maternal abundance or "natural" forms of vampirism. She will not let her child eat her, but something is eating her and she herself cannot stop consuming. We still have to deal with the cemetery, but later.

XIV

First let us spend the night with Madame Bovary. It is a night of devoration and one which—perhaps we have succeeded in demonstrating as much—is not doing "organic food." When does Emma Bovary start doing the artifice for which she officially gets busted? When does she start hallucinating literature? "When she was thirteen her father took her to town to place her in a convent school. They stopped at an inn at the Saint-Cervais quarter where they ate their supper from plates on which scenes from the life of Mademoiselle de la Vallière were painted. The explanatory captions, interrupted here and there by knife scratches, all glorified piety, the sensibilities of the heart and the pomp of the court" (30).

From this point onward, literature presents itself now as an addictive substance, now as a kind of birth control pill, simulating pregnancies of the imagination, keeping the body open to comestible fictions. In any case, as she downs literature, her palate adjusts to these plates with their cutting traces. She consumes literature without end. This, however, always refers her to the possibility of food or its refusal, a kind of symbolic order about which Flaubert remains tenaciously explicit. This supper, in the company of her father, at the threshhold of the convent, may represent her last supper. She was thirteen. Henceforth she would receive other communions, touching off different registers of incorporation. Shortly thereafter, in fact, on one occasion, "she tried to fast for a whole day, to mortify herself" (30).

She is not the only one. Others have a similar rapport to the thing, literature, that they swallow. And so the narrative brings up the addict-supplier, the old spinster, as it was then said of the solitary feminine, who came to the convent to mend linen. A dispossessed aristocrat, she

eat-speak-interiorize

secretly let the older girls read the novels she always had in her apron pocket (the good lady herself devoured [*avalait*] long chapters from them during the intervals in her work). (31)

When she has a good hit of literature Emma experiences "raptures." Flashback. What is going down?

The primary order of depravity on which the novel reports, prior to any loosening of the libidinal bolt, concerns Emma's eating habits, which forms the great metaphoric reserve for everything she takes and rejects. Her appetitive needs are at no point conceived either as natural or conventional, but somewhere between what these categories legislate. In an early outline profiling the sequence of events, Flaubert noted marginally:

Eating disorders

> **Depraved appetites of Mme Bovary, loves unripe fruit, likes her food undercooked, drinks vinegar, and eats pickles for breakfast.**[45]

This would indicate a starting point for reading the tables of her law, the fundamental question of appetite (taste, desire) in its asserted relation to depravity. What does it mean when one refuses to eat properly or according to convention? What is being projected when someone develops bad eating habits? And what about the particularity of Emma Bovary's taste, or any judgment of taste?

Check out the menu; what does it prepare for us?

Resembling the alcoholic who frequently drinks in order to preserve an incorporated other, Emma's depravity consists in favoring the marinated, the preserved, or the object not yet converted to a food substance, a dubious feast of vampiric wonder ("likes her food undercooked").

The trajectivity of the eaten in the novel goes from her father's annual gift of a turkey, intended to celebrate Charles's successful binding of his leg, to her first suicide attempt, which was provoked by a note delivered in a basket of apricots. The basket case came compliments of Rodolphe. He has decided not to share the projected trip with her. This early contiguity of death threat and fruit cocktail that blasts its way through her house forces down her throat the poison that Emma must swallow.

"In times of crises, on TV, someone always resorts to making coffee. Maybe coffee was the right thing at this moment."— *Cookie Mueller*

Sometimes, when you cannot swallow your pride, you take the poison.

Fine. We can no longer accept a thinking by denial, another turn around the block without visiting the cemetery. As we enter this public opening in the novel, we should not recoil but recall that Flaubert likes playing there. It gave him almost as much pleasure as did his father's dissecting theater. The cemetery is linked to a manifest thematics of eating and vampirism through the agency of M. Lestiboudois, who exploits the land of the dead in order to grow potatoes. Potatoes—this dead vegetable, a somewhat inorganic organic fruit, dotted with eyes, blind like the seer of Emma's end—bloat the novel like the gastronomic fillers that they are: morbid accompaniment to meat, they organize a kind of *objet petit a* on the plate of desire. The novel tells us that the experience of eating is implanted in the experience of mourning. This goes for the potato as well as the cold turkey and apricots, Emma's blood stains, his coffee. Who runs this farm of the undead?

"You're feeding on the dead, Lestiboudois!"

If the novel has a plot, it is located in the cemetery. Entering this space—it is public, democratic, you all have access to it—we will discover that there are in effect two bodies lying in wait there, one on which Emma continues symbolically to feed, and another that remote controls her. In fact, they are both parasitically bound to her, but the first body is symbolically rooted in what we might call the *toxic maternal*. We shall examine this body closely, not only because Flaubert delights in fixing the gaze of autopsy but also because this body continues to transmit through Emma the persecutory rules that govern her habits, and hence rule her out. The *toxic maternal* means that while mother's milk is poison, it still supplies the crucial nourishment that the subject seeks. It suggests, moreover, that the maternal is too close, invading the orifices and skin with no screen protection, as it were, no intervening law to sever the ever-pumping umbilicus. This is what it means to find the men surrounding Emma "weak": they are too weak to sever or divert the toxic maternal. It taps back into her own daughter. It recommences. Emma is absorbing medicine that nourishes by poisoning. And this poison still circulates through the textual body, haunting its every move, hunting down the heroine whose phobic maternal fits we have already noted.

XV

When Emma Rouault, bored by the nothingness enveloping her, first met Charles Bovary, she thought she liked him. She was not simply listless, but bored to death. One day the seduction began, and here is what she told her suitor:

On being bored to death

> **She talked to him about her mother and the cemetery, and even showed him the flower bed in the garden from which, on the first Friday of every month, she picked flowers to place on her grave. . . . And, according to what she was saying, her voice was either clear or shrill; or, suddenly becoming languorous, it would trail off into inflections that ended almost in a murmur, as though she were talking to herself. Sometimes her eyes would open wide in guileless joy, then her eyelids would droop while her face took on an expression of profound boredom and her thoughts seemed to wander aimlessly. (19)**

Tightly regimented, the sequencing of a language of seduction centers itself on "her mother and the cemetery," moving toward a kind of murmur of non-address that leaves off on profound boredom. She is bored stiff. In the meantime, the lover's discourse has been held over the abyss of a graveyard, with everything, including eyelids, being pulled by a downward tug in the narrative.

As symptom, boredom is co-originary with melancholia. It pervades everything, and cannot be said simply to erupt. Nor does it desist of its own. It is prior to signification, yet it appears to be a commentary on life; it is, at least for Emma, the place of deepest struggle. It also makes her American: when dialectically tilted, she can be viewed as fun-loving (Flaubert was fascinated with America, and particularly with California). Boredom, with its temporal slowdown and edge of anguish, is also an authentic mode of being-in-the-world. Boredom inflects a sonic quality, it attunes a murmur or an attitude of voice. Infusing the whole text with its ground level of non-sense, Emma's boredom appears to exhaust a certain reserve before it has been tapped.[46] It is companion to loss, but raised on tranquilizers. In *Madame Bovary,* boredom opens a listening to disappearance, fabricating a society's holding pattern over the death that traverses us. It fills the extreme side of passive receptivity, threading through a nothingness which reminds us that Flaubert has wanted nothing more:

> **What I would like to write is a book about nothing at all — almost no subject.**[47]

This forms the threshold through which the existence of Emma Bovary is made to pass, a zone of experience that conspires with "nothing at all," the extenuation of the subject. Something like an ontology of boredom announces its necessity here. We are reminded that for Baudelaire and Gautier, Flaubert's contemporaries and acquaintances, this experience of nothing is at times laced with drugs.[48] Baudelaire names it in *Les Paradis artificiels.*

And even when the life of Emma Bovary erupts periodically into an experience without precedent, it is reappropriated only by means of absorption and inhalation.

Thus the appointed metonymy of the magnificent ball, a cigar box, needs to be taken repeatedly, as an imperious compulsion: "She would look at it, open it and sniff its lining, which was impregnated with an odor of verbena and tobacco" (49).

Living boredom on the outer fringes of hysteria, Emma Bovary accedes to a domestic drug administration:

> **She grew pale and had palpitations of the heart. Charles gave her valerian and camphor baths. Everything he tried seemed to make her more overwrought than ever.**
>
> **There were days when she chattered feverishly for hours on end; and this overexcitement would be abruptly followed by a period of torpor during which she neither spoke nor moved. She would then revive herself by pouring a bottle of eau de Cologne over her arms. (58)**

XVI

It is perhaps now evident that *Madame Bovary* establishes exclusive rights over acts of eating. This perhaps explains why, against the grain of realism, Jonathan Culler has preferred to consider it a "vealist" novel, acknowledging the bovine markers with which it asserts itself.[49] Whatever the nature of the animal or plant applied, ingested, or refused—there exist a great number of scenes of anorectic stubbornness, particularly at times when Emma favors reading over eating—their value remains stable to the extent that they often open a thematics of restoration. So, for example, Monsieur Rouault annually sends a turkey as a commemorative gift. Restoring the other—the origin of all restaurants—implies that food substance, like the pharmakon, possesses the power to kill or put away. Hence the apricots and coffee.

There is nothing more constant and increasingly uncanny than human feeding time. This fact has occurred to all literatures everywhere, setting out from the Homeric feast to Goethe's *table d'hôte* and Kafka's judgment seats around the family table. But Emma eats, as it were, between meals and what she eats when eating is an enigmatic substance by means of which she succeeds in internalizing the potato chips of mourning. In some respects she joins the lineage begun by Cinderella, who eats cinders in the wake of a toxic mother, projected and tripled by stepmother and sisters. The toxic mother, when absent, is remembered tenderly but recast materially into evil substitutes. Where Cinderella was saved by the ball and recognized by the princely Other, lifted above mourning and destitution, Cinderemma, for her part, experiences the same ballroom scene. Her insertion into the rush of otherness is followed by the pain of expulsion, though with no return. She has a carriage, too, and when it takes off, it rocks along like a tomb. And her pumpkin retrieves a miniaturized if poisoned echo in an apricot. As for the fitting shoes, nothing befits Emma—Flaubert shows off her tendency to walk through manure and mud.[50] (In fact, Charles complains at the ball that *his* shoes do not fit.) As with Cinderella, something that only a saving empire could disengage keeps pulling her down. Indeed, the novel traces a downward movement, as if the gravity of the cemetery were holding on to her feet.

Something is eating at Madame Bovary. She has a "depraved appetite," which is to say, she accepts as comestible what by natural or normed evaluation ought to be refused. Intricate parasitism. Something is eating at Madame Bovary. And her "depraved appetite" suggests that she doubles for this other. How is eating, this metonymy of introjection, to be understood? It is important to figure this out, for devouring, reading, swallowing, and suicide are linked as one great train rushing through the novel's underground. It is surely no longer necessary to thematize Freud's observations on mourning, which by now have become easy to swallow.

> **The ego wants to incorporate this object into itself, and, in accordance with the oral or cannibalistic phase of libidinal development in which it is, it wants to do so by devouring it.[51]**

On a losing streak, threatened by impoverishment and ruin, the ego wants to incorporate "this object" into itself—an act that involves, but also always exceeds, the materiality of eating. Between devouring the other and sticking to food substance, there exists another possibility for mourning the lost object. It is offered with dessert. Linked to eating, it appears however to mark a complement to Emma's endless absorption and cannibalistic dependency. The other mode of mourning the lost one is quick and spontaneous, punctuating the end of a meal. In this service, the cadaverous presence is downed in a moment, thereafter extinguished. We are at the end of a meal.

It comes as no great shock perhaps that it is upon Charles Bovary to represent the promise of sudden and successful mourning. This follows a prescription for fast food temporality, zipping by the bereaved memory of his first wife.

> **Charles surprised himself by laughing, but he was sobered when the memory of his wife came back to him. Then coffee was served and he stopped thinking about her. (18)**

There is little in the way of alcoholic or melancholic trace in Charles. The corpse slips away, carried by the liquid that anticipates and doubles the ink deposit that his second wife will spit up. Here coffee serves as liquid eraser, where memory returns momentarily in order to be washed away all the more robustly. Madame Bovary's body count is more subtle and hence more difficult to pin down and evacuate.

If Charles and Emma Bovary can be viewed as constituting a couple, they divide their properties over the difference between melancholia and mania. Emma indeed exhibits the vital signs of melancholia in the sense that a retentive agency appears to hold on to the figures which threaten to slip away. The melancholic preserves what is otherwise devoured, assimilated, and expelled by mourning. Charles's burst of laughter, on the other hand, intervenes at table to punctuate mania. In truth, mania alternates with melancholia. "Mania," writes Laurence Rickels, "confirms by reversing this retentive tendency of melancholia."

Mania and Melancholia

> **A "festival of liberation" according to Abraham, mania celebrates the ego's sudden triumph over both ego ideal and the once-loved, lost, and subsequently introjected object. Whereas in melancholia the ego is vampirized by the introjected object, in mania the libido turns with ravenous hunger to the external world of objects; whatever appears before the manic's rapidly advancing probe is swallowed. But this pleasurable swallowing during the manic phase, which succeeds the melancholic's sense that he is excluded from the world of objects as though disinherited, corresponds to an equally rapid, equally pleasurable expulsion of the briefly retained objects and impressions.[52]**

Flaubert, however, co-intricates mania and melancholia by multiplying the losses and shattering the unity of the object. I would like to connect this broken structure to two haunting losses deposited into the folds of *Madame Bovary*. We have already suggested the presence of a toxic mother who supplants a lover's discourse, blocking satisfaction while demanding ever more absorption: a clandestine pact destined to maintain an impossible conservation.[53] Something is growing in Emma of which the repelled child, Berthe, is a symptom. Inhabited by this other, parasited by its demand, the subject cannot let it pass. The other in its absence must somehow be kept alive and preserved; this requires certain metonymies of feeding. To retain the other, the subject, wanting to satisfy its depraved hunger, follows a foreign regime, filling an emptiness that somehow leaves the subject full. The body becomes the site for exercising the rights of a missing person. This person or parasite, as interiorized other, is imperious. It demands immediate satisfaction of a felt lack. What are we calling "it"? How does its constitution, at the limits of materiality, reveal itself, and under what conditions? By now we have traveled along the body of mania and melancholia to its addictive recesses. This body, the body of the addict, invents a supplementary organ which discloses itself particularly in moments of abstinence, the negative complement to a fiction of immediate satisfaction. In abstinence, the addicted subject radically encounters the phantasm of lack. It has fabricated and textured an organ implant that requires absolute attention in the mode of care. Thus abstinence aggravates and accelerates the relation to lack, disclosing terrific contours. There's no giving up the other.

XVII

Abstinence—cold turkey—opens the medusoid rift. It—cold turkey—has to be stuffed or sutured, sometimes by a diluted form of itself. An orifice, skin opens to introduce a foreign body, a liquifying phallus. While there is nothing to prevent the phallus from being maternal, in Emma's case we can discern an additional twist in the umbilicus. She has a double vacancy to occupy her. Therefore, when

Emma Bovary offers signs of phallic consistency, this does not occur as a simple episode of gender drifting, but as an inscription made by a foreign body gendered otherwise. Beyond the scattered marks of virility duly noted by Flaubert scholars, one can put on her account signs of an anally organized arousal which, somewhat understandably, have not received much note. Her link to Charles is first libidinized when:

> **She saw it and bent down over the sacks. He gallantly hurried over to her, and as they both reached down at the same time he felt his chest graze her back, which was curved beneath him. She straightened up, blushing deeply, and looked at him over her shoulder as she handed him his riding crop. (14)**

Another inflection of this primal scene of desire returns in their married life when:

> **Emma would be in her room, combing her hair; he would tiptoe up to her and kiss her from behind; she would cry out in surprise. (29)**

On being paranoid and maybe homosexual.

These instituting surprise attacks when she is reversed, that is to say, neither entirely male nor female and yet both, suggest a double contract that grants sexual mobility. It is as if she were preparing the grounds for anal sadistic pleasure sites from a place of identification with a virilely gendered other. She may be surprised, but the novel severally infers her incorporation of a male homosexual libido. Sure, she resists this identification, she blushes and cries out, but what do you think it means to exist in a paranoid text? It means you are supposed to be surprised, shocked, disgusted, resistant, and in denial.[54] There is something to her reversibility and the way she dominates Charles after their wedding night that suggests an intrafold. Or perhaps, too, there is something in the resolute determination with which she makes of Léon "her mistress" (240), as it is said, or when she is said to be or look like a man, that plies her addiction with a supplement of desire. Her libido is manned, we could say, by a boy on the loose, while her addictive structure originates in the toxic maternal. Flaubert prepares the double occupancy of Madame Bovary's body textually with the double-featured Madame Bovarys preceding Emma's appearance in the novel, as well as with the dividing marks of internal otherness that she periodically reflects. Emma Bovary arrives as supplementary to the novel whose primary figure she represents. This is not to say that, prior to these contaminations, there ever existed the possibility for a pure distillation down to the essence of Emma—even though she herself dreams of virginal erasure and practices rites of mortification. On the contrary, these practices indicate purity as something to be *added* to a self already in progress, exposed to the other who serves as an inscription machine of sorts.

The other co-habiting Emma has a double origin in the novel: his virtual presence is mediated by fiction and by paternal law. For it is through her father's mouth that the missing other emerges. In a classically literary scene Father, like Claudius, teaches his not quite kin, Charles, a lesson on mourning and what remains left over. His teaching coincides with the moment he wishes to acquit himself of a debt and pay Charles for setting his once broken leg—a settling of accounts that will be cruelly doubled and annulled by a subsequent leg operation that sets Charles's legacy.

"One morning M. Rouault brought Charles his payment for setting his broken leg: seventy-five francs in two-franc coins, plus a turkey. He had learned of his loss, and he consoled him as best he could."

"I know how it is," he said, patting him on the shoulder. "I've gone through the same thing myself. After I lost my poor wife I used to go out into the fields to be alone. . . . I was almost out of my mind. I couldn't eat, and even the thought of going to a café made me feel sick—you can't imagine how it was! Well, gradually, with one day

coming after another, with a spring after a winter and a fall on top of a summer, I got over it, little by little, bit by bit. It went away, vanished; or, rather, it sank out of sight, because there's always something left, something like a weight that you carry around inside you, here, in your chest! But sooner or later it will happen to all of us, so you musn't let yourself waste away; there's no sense in wanting to die just because someone else is dead! You must pull yourself together, Monsieur Bovary; you'll get over it!"(17)

The lesson, nuanced but clear, promises Charles that he will overcome the loss; at the same time, however, it asserts the permanent lesion caused by the loss. It vanished but did not completely disappear, a remnant lodged itself in him, which he continues to carry like a weight. Vanishing, it still weighs in periodically, disappearing and reappearing with the transferential movement of his language, always throwing a lifeline to the other with whom the carrier identifies: like a weight that *you* carry ("car il vous reste toujours quelque chose au fond" [54]).

This *reste* or residue which never rests but rather sinks out of sight to return again, takes two to carry. The message is double, revealing the ever doubled bind of a true mourning which would claim fully to do away with the other. But Charles instantly forgets the residue, receiving the lesson instead like a command that orders him fully to reappropriate the other, leaving nothing behind. Obeying a logic of instantaneous capacities, he manages to vaporize the corpse over coffee. Taking another sip,

Charles surprised himself by laughing, but he was sobered when the memory of his wife came back to him. Then coffee was served and he stopped thinking about her. (18)

Shortly thereafter, when Charles successfully evacuates the one in exchange for the other Madame Bovary, Monsieur Rouault turns into a kind of missing persons bureau and suffers a hit of melancholia. He has become solitary guardian of the patronymic as Emma slips into Bovary. Giving away his daughter, he remembers his own wedding, which evokes in turn another departed child: "Their son would now be thirty if he were still alive! He looked back again and saw nothing on the road. He felt desolate and dreary, like an empty, deserted house, and as tender memories and gloomy thoughts mingled in his mind, which was still beclouded by vapors of the feast, he had a momentary impulse to head toward the church" (26). Here as elsewhere in the novel Flaubert emphasizes a link between melancholia and a mind dispersed in vapors. His irony annexes the other opiate—the other empty house—to scenes of depressed spirits, the church, which Monsieur Rouault decides against visiting. Paternal law is falling down.

a. paternal law

XVIII

In a crucial chapter following Emma's disillusionment with marriage—life did not coincide with what fabulation had promised—Emma reverts to fiction. She recalls the beginnings of her hallucinatory reading list, which offers the first mention in the novel of the necessity of books. Prior to the organization of her literary plates, at the beginning of chapter six, Emma is busy translating her father's nostalgia into a fictional genealogy. This translation enables her to circumscribe a lost object without naming it, momentarily lighting up a subterranean path of grief. Translating her father's pain into fiction, Emma recuperates little brother, abandoning the deserted house for fields of the imaginary. The naive plenitude of the mood she attunes offers a landscape directed by a powerfully generous God. The missing brother is relocated to *Paul and Virginia:*

b. fiction

> **She had read *Paul and Virginia* and dreamed of the bamboo cabin, the Negro Domingo and the dog Fidèle, and especially of the sweet friendship of a devoted little brother who would climb trees higher than a steeple to pick red fruit for her, or run barefoot across the sand, bringing her a bird's nest. (30)**

Where Monsieur Rouault counts the years of absence and abstinence, Madame Bovary restores the missing sibling to the continual field of fiction, dreaming the repetition of absolute, if problematically coded, fidelity. Literature produces effects of lived experience.

To love literature.

We soon learn, following the beginning of her mimetic excess—her fast identifications and novel devorations—that for "six months, at the age of fifteen, Emma soiled her hands with this dust from old lending libraries. Later, with Sir Walter Scott, she developed a passion for things historical and dreamed of wooden chests . . ." (32). It would be hasty to suppose that we already know what it means to love literature, to be a bibliophile or to feel comfortable in libraries. There is little doubt that, whether by institutional transmission or private pleasure, letters revive what is dead because they work not so much from this side of life but as mummified objects responsible for transports and identification. To this extent they obey a pharmacologic. From *Macbeth* to *Dorian Gray,* literature has literalized its effects through a syntax of casting spells and charms, opening a region of nonknowledge in unceasing negotiation with finitude. For Emma Bovary, spellbound by the books she reads, things are constantly given over to serial mummification:

> **As for the memory of Rodolphe, she had pushed it down to the bottom of her heart, and it lay there as still and solemn as the mummy of a pharaoh in an underground burial chamber. (185)[55]**

Truly her father's daughter, she has become the construction site for a crypt into which she deposits her lovers. Yet the crypt is cracked and something that borders upon substance seeps out:

> **This great embalmed love gave off a fragrance which seeped through everything and perfumed with tenderness the immaculate atmosphere in which she was striving to live. (185)**

Remains of this love revive a minimal trace of materiality, a vapor permeating everything, escaping and leaking into the blank zone associated with Emma's still life. It is the trace-gas signaling the undead. The narrative imputes movement to a dead love that nonetheless stirs. The blanket of immobile precision covers Emma, and not Rodolphe—or rather, the "memory of Rodolphe." This memory tenders something that is inhaled.

Vague deposits of incense and opiate fumes construct the love crypt which sublimates smoothly into religious phantasmagoria.[56] That which is left of the embalmed love returns in the form of the living sacred. The narrative signals the internal religious wars that come to mark a displaced pharmaceutical desire, for "the dresser, its top cluttered with medicine bottles, was transformed into an altar" (184). In the crucial playoffs between representatives of pharmacy and of religion, the priest declares music to be less dangerous to morals than literature: "The pharmacist sprang to the defense of letters" (188).

It is not fortuitous that the druggist comes to the support of the simulacrum, the pharmakon. He has offered Emma the unlimited use of his library, inviting the addicted neighbor to mix pharmaceuticals and literature. "'Of course,' continued Homais, 'there's bad literature, just as there's bad pharmacy'" (188). Literature comes down on the side of pharmacy, if somewhat negatively cast. Religion, which also deals in transcendental experience, appears to opt for the non-mimetic trance, which is why music is viewed as safe text. According to the priest, literature would be the gathering place around which sexual difference, simulacra, make-up, and effeminacy are decisively organized.

> **"I know very well," objected the priest, "that there are good literary works and good authors. But all those people of different sex gathered in a luxurious room decorated with all sorts of worldly splendor, and the pagan disguises, the make-up, the bright lights, the effeminate voices—those things alone are enough to create a licentious frame of mind and give rise to evil thoughts and impure temptations." (188)**

Flaubertian irony adds this gestural move: "'And if the Church condemned the theater,' he added, suddenly assuming a mystical tone as he rolled himself a pinch of snuff, 'she must have good reason for it. We must submit to her decrees'" (188). Relinquishing literature, Monsieur le priest nonetheless inhales his stimulating substance and powders his nose.

Repeating and distorting the Kantian aesthetic, the text says that literary forms (and not the literary content or signified) liberate the mind to its utmost capacities. The theatrical frame and parergonal indices alone produce a desiring frame of mind. Literature stages appearance and libidinal encounter; it originates need.

Léon hesitated.

XIX

"'Of course,' continued Homais, 'there's bad literature, just as there's bad pharmacy.'" Bad pharmacy well exposes the allegory of dissolution to which Emma Bovary's relationship with Léon succumbs. Their encounter begins and ends with mediated pharmacy. Habitually, she would go to see him on Thursdays. In Rouen.

Timed release

One day the pharmacist calamitously invades their Thursday with the expectation that Léon might divert him. Emma in the hotel room, expecting Léon to divert her: "Léon hesitated, as though struggling against the pharmacist's spell" (243). Homais puts him in a trance, immobilizes him where Emma stimulates, exhausts him. He cannot cut it, "Léon hesitated."

Emma had begun to poison his life; the pharmacist casts a spell. Caught between the charm and the poison, Léon yields to the spell of the pharmacy. The blow is struck, and each member of the couple chooses a drug. Emma, for her part, will try to recuperate the couple's losses by dispensing letters whose effects are intended to pump up the fiction of desire. As if to underscore her experience of craving for external supplements, the narrative alerts us to the "naive expedients of a weakened passion trying to stimulate itself by external means" (244). These refer to the letters she henceforth sends to him, or rather the letters that send her, for they arouse the hope that "her next trip would bring her profound bliss" (244). The addicted body slips something between them:

> **And yet, in that forehead covered with beads of cold sweat, in those stammering lips, those wild eyes and those clutching arms, Léon felt the presence of something mad, shadowy and ominous, something that seemed to be subtly slipping between them, as though to separate them. (244)**

If Léon's thoughts appear to be capable of exceptional lucidity, this is not because they are inspired by a mood of sobriety. He, for his part, gets caught in the negativity of failing abstinence:

> **He even tried to force himself to stop loving her, but as soon as he heard her footsteps he would feel helplessly weak, like a drunkard at the sight of liquor. (244)**

Poison and alcohol. Emma kicks in, like a drug circulating alongside the prescriptive precincts of pharmacy. Léon loses his grip, his job is coming apart, time and money condense. Ever since their carriage ride he can't stay on the wagon. The encapsulated vehicle soon yielded to hard liquor. He can't let go. When compared with Emma, the pharmacist possesses a certain charm.

Destroyed by the one, Léon is held spellbound by the other. Marked as illicit and harmful, Emma Bovary belongs to the domain of books. While Léon grows increasingly more desperate and weak, Emma takes recourse in those "naive expedients," external supplements. He disintegrates. Meanwhile, her rapport to him benefits from the coherency of delirium. She is the hallucinator. Emma, she had longed for the "ineffable sentiments of love which she had tried to imagine from her books!" (245).

> **The first months of her marriage, her rides in the forest, her waltzes with the viscount, Lagardy singing—everything passed before her eyes. . . . (245)**

But her hallucinations are gapped. They are connected to longing and to a certain knowledge of what is not there. The delirium stops short, breaking open the distance. Unable to coincide with the books she's consumed, he will never answer to the hysteric's demand for eternity. It cracks: "And Léon suddenly appeared to her as remote as the others" (245).

Distance has asserted itself not as an enabling condition for love or thought, but as punishment. He joins the procession of the phantomal others. She cannot go into withdrawal. She will increase the dosages, accelerate the need, in order to gather up what

can

not

be

had.

"Why was life so unsatisfying? Why did everything she leaned on instantly crumble into dust?" (245). And here we find the suturing lament, the dispersal of support into dust, the crumbling other that she was to consume incessantly, as dust, in part because something—she calls it life—was relentlessly insistent upon withholding what might have satisfied her. Here we might suggest that the distinction, so rigorously maintained in the Hegelian Lacan, between need and desire, may be the luxury of the sober.

Doctor's Report

COL: 01-
DIS: ________
FAM:

E. Bovary's downfall was neither gradual nor unmotivated. There is even a professor from Berkeley, California, who claims to have discovered the double source of her death drive: the two-chambered crypt built around the lost mother and brother of Emma Bovary. While we do not care to dispute this conclusion, neither are we inclined to take into consideration fanciful arguments construed by literature professors. It is our task only to confirm that Ms. Bovary suffered incalculable damage as a result of her husband's egregious admittance to the field of medicine. There is no doubt in our minds that Charles Bovary carried the stain of his father's irresponsible professional engagement. As Dr. Lacan has noted, every subject belongs to a circuit that transmits error and secrecy from one generation to the next. Like Faust before him, Charles Bovary was the beneficiary of a history of corruption in medical practice. Our records show that his father, Monsieur Charles-Denis-Bartholomé Bovary had once been an assistant surgeon in the army. He was "forced to leave the service in 1812 for corrupt practices with regard to conscription" (3). Charles Bovary, however, was no Faust. He was filled to satisfaction with the knowledge he felt himself to have attained. So ignorant was he that his wife, asking for the meaning of a word she had come across in one of her many novels, was obliged to realize that "this man taught nothing" (135). In our estimation, and after lengthy deliberation, this complacency of the mediocre in itself may have sufficed to charge him with willfully inducing the destruction of his legal companion. Faced with the *béance* of a non-teaching, a full blockage in the transmission of knowledge, a distension of transferential activity upon which all healthy contact is founded, Ms. Bovary had nowhere to turn. It is clear to us that she was an exceptionally talented woman who experienced difficulty, due to primary identificatory processes, in distinguishing between the *Innen* and *Aussenwelt* (Dr. Freud). We dispute recent reports of her regression to the oral cannibalistic libido while it is evident to us that she sought the phallus in the desire of the Other. However, the Other had the indecency of disappearing, which led Ms. B. to endless attempts at restoring it to the function of an object of imaginary incorporation.

Ms. B.'s psyche was disposed to drug dependency at an early age. It was made clear to her from the start, however, that she would have to wait until the next century in order properly to shoot up. The crucial catastrophe that led her to assume a full posture of substance dependency occurred when Gustave Flaubert laced the novel with a fatal autobiographical injection. Mr. Flaubert was not himself in control of the substance he administered; however, it dealt the fatal blow to Emma B. Discharging his poison upon her, Mr. Flaubert was henceforth free to indulge in hallucinatory trances that he habitually termed "writing." It might be added, for the sake of scientific objectivity, that Flaubert frequented notoriously dubious characters: a Baudelaire, a Gautier, and not the least of all, his own mistress, a woman of loose and reprobate character, a poet, and at one time the lover of the philosopher and statesman Victor Cousin. Her child, Henrietta, was not fathered by her legal husband. Additionally, we have noted Mr. Flaubert's addictive intimacies with Alfred Le Poittevin, whom he incorporated, and subsequently with Louis Bouilhet who virtually dictated the particulars of Flaubert's oeuvre.

It was at a moment when Mr. Flaubert was performing in the novel a double oedipal bypass that all Ms. B.'s hopes were dashed. The operation was a complete success for Mr. Flaubert; it destroyed the heroine definitively. As a result of the absolute infighting of medicine and pharmacy, when everything was staked on the resurrection of a third leg, the heroine was made to enter a strategic zone that declared her loser. We owe thanks here to Professor Harry Levin, formerly of Harvard University, for signaling "the parallel lives of the author and the heroine, daily, weekly, monthly, yearly." Dr. Levin justly refers to Emma B.'s disposition of mind as *hallucination.* His researches have led him to diagnose "this narcissistic attitude of Emma's, this self-hallucination induced by over-reading." (Our staff is currently investigating the etiology of self-hallucination and over-reading.) Dr. Levin goes on to underscore the patient's hallucinatory propensities: "Imaginative effort was reinforced by documentation when Flaubert sought the proper shading for Emma's hallucinations by immersing himself in *Keepsakes* and other feminine periodicals. By plying his brother with queries about surgery and toxicology, he filled in the peculiar symptoms his outline required: 'Agony: precise medical details' 'on the morning of the twenty-third she had vomiting spells again. . . .'"[57]

Our investigations indicate that Fl.'s dependency upon his brother at the moment he develops toxicological theories will prove fatal. Emma B., whose own brother had disappeared, is faced with an operation unconsciously dominated by Fl.'s brother (clearly superimposed upon the paternal function) in a struggle among surgical caresses the intensity of which makes Cain and Abel seem naive. We intend to demonstrate first that this operation involves oedipal structures, and that it also implies a fraternal rift.

The entire scene originates in a scheme concocted by the neighboring apothecary, Mr. Homalis. Exposed as the drama of the signifier par excellence, the critical operation comes down to a young man's *clubfoot.* The oedipal showdown commences with the instigating utterance, offered by the apothecary, "Are you a man or not?" (151). Equally noxious was the provocation, "After all, what's there to lose?" (150). Indeed, the answer to the second question obtains in the stakes mounted by the first question. All the loose ends, the bruises and errors converge in the place of a botched operation. This was Emma B.'s last chance for scoring on sublimation, displacement, and pride. Ever looking "to have something more solid than love to lean on" (150), Emma is willing to invest the future of her husband's career psychically. But the future for Emma B. arrives as a modified form of the concealed past. The crypt formation, concretized and exteriorized, is prepared on the model of "a kind of box weighing about eight pounds" (151) that was fitted to the leg of a young man, a certain Hippolyte. The crypt-effect attending the operation is intensified further by the materiality of the bandages, "a whole pyramid of bandages—the apothecary's entire stock" (152). The intense cooperation of medicine, crypt, and pharmacy held out the last hope, it was meant to give Emma B. something more solid than love to lean on. The operation was performed as per recipe, by a mimetics of the real that forms the other side of Emma B.'s identificatory hallucinations. The burial plot thickens. "Urged on by the apothecary and Emma, Charles agreed to go through with it. He sent to Rouen for Dr. Duval's book and buried himself in it every night, holding his head between his hands" (151). That this activity needed to be understood as an operation on the signifier, and hence as allegory of naming, was abundantly indicated "in other words": "*strephocatopodia, strephenopodia* and *strephexopodia* (or, to put it more clearly, deviations of the foot downward, inward or outward), along with *strephypopodia* and *strephanopodia* (downward or upward torsion)" (151).

"You'll feel nothing more than a very slight pain at the most; it's just a prick, like a little bloodletting"

The cut and inscription however can be made only on the name that ligates the brother to the father's place—"Charles would have to cut the Achilles tendon, leaving the anterior tibial muscle to be taken care of later, to cure the varus, for he was afraid to risk two operations at once" (152). Gustave Flaubert, for his part, was not afraid to risk two operations at once. His brother and sometime rival, the surgeon, succeeded by supplanting the father, who had also been his sometime rival. His name, repeating that of the father, was Achille Flaubert. The crucial operation was therefore serially double: literature operating on medicine, Flaubert on Achilles, Homais on Emma, Emma on Charles, Charles on Clubfoot (Oedipus), Charles on Emma, Emma on Flaubert. What is at issue involves the becoming of man. In French the inflation of a letter renders the proper name of the cut more pronounced than in English: "il fallait couper le tendon d'Achille . . . car le médecin n'osait d'un seul coup risquer deux opérations" (205).

In the real life of Gustave Flaubert, Achille tended to the upper part of his father's leg. Dr. Flaubert had mentioned a pain in his thigh. After Achille operated, the good doctor endured the agonies of infection and gangrene before death ensued as the consequence of his son's surgical manipulations. Only a short while later, the beloved sister, Caroline, began to expire. Caroline, whose pregnancy at that time had been without any complication whatsoever, had come to Rouen during her father's illness. She gave birth six days after his death. After several weeks chills and a temperature began to appear; it was puerperal fever. Following a period of dramatic suffering, she died.

These two deaths, upon which Flaubert comments copiously in his letters, created among other things the symbolic displacements by which Fl. and his mother formed the parental unit that brought up Caroline's child. To his mother (who was to become the place of the writing habit) he promised himself:

I care nothing for the world, for the future, for what people will say, for any kind of established position, or even for literary fame, which in my early days I used to stay awake so many nights dreaming about. That is what I am like; that is my character. No, no; when I think of your sweet face, so sad, so loving, and of the joy I have in living with you, who are so full of serenity, so full of a serious, grave kind of charm, I know very well that I shall never love another as I do you. You will never have a rival, never fear! The senses or the fancy of a moment will not take the place of that which lies enclosed *in triple sanctuary.* Some will perhaps mount to the threshold of the temple, but none will enter. (Letter to his mother from Constantinople December 15, 1850; italics added)

These are some of the operations, "in triple sanctuary," to which Fl. submitted his destiny as well as that of his heroine. The after-effects and consequences of the Achilles intervention were indeed endlessly spiraling around oedipal configurations. It was not long before Fl., incorporating and cryptaphorizing, became post-oedipal.

As for the inscribed couple, on the fragile eve of their second honeymoon, over this body whose Achilles tendon has not yet erupted in its sheer unmasterability—as for this couple, "they sat down to table; he ate heartily and even asked for a cup of coffee with his dessert, a dissolute pleasure which he allowed himself only on Sundays when there was company" (153). Ah, but there was company, the reemerging phantoms inscribed by the operation on the clubfoot. Charles B., for his part, took the toxic of forgetting that night, administering to himself a substance that had at one time induced the corpse of the second Madame Bovary to slip away. As with the primal scene of forgetting the reproachful body (he turned away, she died), coffee, a dissolute pleasure, brings up the haunting image of black liquid. The toxic spill of the suicidal mark comes up in the site of the mutilated phallus: "A livid tumescence ran up the leg, and scattered over it were pustules from which a black liquid was oozing. The case had taken a serious turn" (155). Gangrene catches hold of the invaded body, rushes up his leg to the

"eyes full of terror, sobbing, stammering"

belly. Disconnecting and disconnecting. The conspiracy of medicine and religion collapses: "Meanwhile religion seemed to be helping him no more than surgery: the invincible gangrene continued to rise toward the belly" (156). We hold in reserve details of subsequent atrocities performed upon the leg that was to have supplied manhood.

It was quite an event in the village, that leg amputation. (157)

Against the pain of this impossible operation the mind begins to alter. Charles, for his part, goes quickly. The drunk arises as a defense against medicine. "Charles looked at her with the clouded eyes of a drunken man as he listened to the amputee's last screams; they came in a succession of long, varied tones interspersed with short, fitful shrieks, like the howling of some animal being slaughtered far away"(160).

In sum, our commission has found the operating theater to generate the exciting cause, the event of no return for Emma B. Where Fl. has thought to exorcise his private Achilles' phantoms, he has in truth reinserted the call of the phantom in the house of Bovary. Henceforth she would be reincorporating the loosened Other according to the exigencies of "intoxication." Faced with the event of no return, her mind is about to alter according to the semantic bifurcation that adultery convenes. Emma B. turns to painkillers. Fl.'s interjections are precise and to the point—

her dreams fallen into the mud like wounded swallows . . . Collapsing under the furious onslaughts of her pride. She revelled in all the malicious ironies of triumphant adultery. The memory of her lover came back to her with intoxicating charm . . . and Charles seemed as detached from her life, as permanently departed, as impossible and annihilated as though he were on the point of death, gasping his last before her eyes. (159–60)

The wound precedes everything; or, at least the theater of impossible operations stages the turn toward the external supplement. Emma B. buys the prosthesis for Hippolyte, ending the drama of the oedipal operation with a wooden leg. From this point onward she became a supplier and user of the artificial prosthesis.

Emma B. continued limply to live on, soon discovering the rush of capital from the local junkie, M. Lheureux: "Emma abandoned herself to this easy way of satisfying all her whims" (163). She "remained under the influence of a kind of idiotic infatuation . . . a blissful torpor; and her soul, sinking into that intoxication, shriveled and drowned like the Duke of Clarence in his butt of malmsey." Her "everyday behaviour changed; she even had the audacity to talk with Rodolphe in public with a cigarette in her mouth." (165).

For his part, "Charles had not followed [his mother's] advice about forbidding Emma to read novels" (166). She goes into convulsions because of an apricot basket.

NURSE'S REPORT: Somehow they had stopped feeding her. Each time, their departure seemed sudden. Demanding satisfaction from life was her big mistake. "Naive," as Mr. Flaubert would say, and temporally misleading. We'd known this disposition since Faust and all the megarock stars beginning with Goethe. There was nothing that would intervene to institute distance or superego; the law of the father was out of working order, which is why she could not abide deferral or denial. In a way, she took the route of every belle âme in the ward. Living the fusional desire, she was exposed to the toxic maternal, en route to dust and dissolution. But where the belle âme strengthens on the ineffable, transcending even the rude materiality of books, Emma B. madly demanded that the ineffable satisfy her, that it go to the encounter with life.

PART SIX : COLD TURKEY
OR, THE TRANSCENDENTAL
AESTHETIC OF THE THING
TO BE EATEN

Installation .01 *In a Thanatorium, metabolist decor, the sonic blare of neon lights, not too bright, buzzing in constant conjugation with translucent walls. Different channels, wind tunnels.*

ERNST JÜNGER: I considered engaging a total mobilization of spirit.

MARTIN HEIDEGGER: Nobody talks that way anymore. At least put quotation marks on spirit.

JACQUES DERRIDA: Don't get hooked on spirit. All these quotation marks are so many signs of being hooked.

HEIDEGGER: Sometimes I withdraw the quotation marks, but they're like vampiric bites, they leave traces and, anyway, it's hard to get off spirit.

DERRIDA: I see. But you do recognize the spectral supplement, don't you, the way we've swished from spirit to spirits. That can't be merely an accident. (*Looking around.*) This place is still too metaphysical for me. Can't you ventilate this textual space?

HEIDEGGER: You French are so fast. Your velocities overwhelm me. I'll never forget that high speed drive with Lacan in the country. It nearly freaked out my wife. He refused to slow down. But you have to slow down, we all do, thinking takes time, *its* time. I'm going back to Aristotle. Why don't you stay?

DERRIDA: There's something about this thanatopos that seems too, how shall I say, scientific to me. Anyway, you're the guy who says science doesn't think. Listen, I'll call you. Stay cool. I've gotta run.

JÜNGER: Check you out later.

HEIDEGGER: Take it slow.

Installation .02 *Another channel. Café across from Hölderlin's herbeceuticals shop. The patronne, knitting a red sweater, switches on the radio, periodically adjusting the volume. This frequently runs interference with the conversations of the customers. Music from* India Song, *a slowly rotating ventilator.*

MARGUERITE FAUST: He got me pregnant and then he left me.

MARGUERITE DURAS: I'm the last one to be cynical on that subject. But, still, it happens often. I'm sorry he left you. It seems to have made you fragile. Why didn't you get an abortion, instead of making such an operatic fuss over the matter and letting Gounod get a piece of the action?

M. FAUST: I couldn't get an abortion. Anyway, my brother scared me and I drowned the kid, so I did exercise a choice option.

DURAS: You are so very naive, so *German*. I say this as someone who has had a German lover, to the extent that you can at all "have" a lover in these cataclysmic times.

M. FAUST: I hear you. I guess I mean to share something a little different with you. At that time I couldn't have an abortion because I had to transfer my entire libido to a religious account.

DURAS: Your entire libido? This is German idealism, my dear. How utterly charming! It would not be so charming in a man, I assure you. Before you knew it, he would be practicing Dasein's virility in Being-towards-death. But wouldn't you say that horror is rather *in* Being, and not in some frightfully heroic encounter with nothingness? Oh, I've interrupted you. Do go on, my dear.

M. FAUST: Well, yes, there is a certain "il y a" of horror that belongs already to Being. You don't have to go looking for nothingness to experience anguish. It's already there.

DURAS: Yes. Even though Martin liked to insist on the generosity of Being, the donations of the "es gibt" which, by the way, have given me so little. I find primordial indebtedness tiresome. I am growing weary of gifts that surpass my initiative. Mind you, I am not reverting to the Subject, I'm just saying that there has been a lot of trouble in that area.

M. FAUST: I think you've gotten off rather well, compared to me. Though I don't want to minimize what you've been through, the atrocious war in which I think my boyfriend had his part. It upsets me to think he's had such a good reputation when he's truly a demon.

DURAS: Well, people admire him, I suppose, for bypassing contained knowledge and control room epistemologies. But you're quite right, he was a monstrous technologue, at least, and one can hardly muster the courage to resist such a character. Mary Shelley quite adored him, though she and her boyfriend managed to get the spectral dimension right.

M. FAUST: I like the way you've always defended Mitterand, your sense of loyalty from the days of the resistance. His name always meant something special to me, even though I'm not exactly a socialist. It designates in my language both the center and the margin. That's what I keep on negotiating myself. I hate politics, don't you?

DURAS: You sound like a little girl. Still, you're not wrong. Hannah used to say to me that the personal is the political. She was complicated. A lot of people are still hard on her because she slept with Martin.

M. FAUST: So? I slept with Faust! Does that make me stupid?

DURAS: I'm afraid it did, at least in terms of the way people are reading you. I hate to tell you this, honey, but Friedrich found you a cultural embarrassment.

M. FAUST: Who's Friedrich?

DURAS: You know, Elisabeth's brother.

M. FAUST: How could anyone related to her have anything worthwhile to say about me?

DURAS: Well, his values are OK. He really hated his sister, especially after what she did to Lou. Tell me, how did you get yourself into such a mess? And then that pathetic display of Christian ecstasy you put on! Who put you up to it?

M. FAUST: It wasn't at all a put on. I really wanted purity, and I thought the infinitizing promise of his discourse would work. Of course I was aware of the flaws in the performative structure of promising—hey, wasn't it Nietzsche who said man was the promising animal? Well, I can tell you that my Faust was definitely that, an animal, a promising animal.

DURAS: But didn't Jean-Luc tell you to be careful about infinite promises and the promise of the infinite?

M. FAUST: I guess so. He said to start from absolute finitude. He made it sound like it was real important. I wasn't sure I could handle finitude, but boy was infinity ever worse! It wasn't really my fault, though, I was trapped in, like, oppositional logic.

DURAS: How's that?

M. FAUST: You know, good and evil, male/female, angel/devil, desire/chastity, knowledge/innocence—all those weird pairs that everyone's been getting amped out about.

DURAS: It wasn't that simple, was it? Don't forget you were Goethe's girl, too, and he kept you off limits from the gang of the eternal feminine. Remember?

M. FAUST: Maybe so. But don't you forget that I was basically hanging with a junkie.

DURAS: What do you mean?

M. FAUST: Faust had the devil on his back. It was the season of the witch. He'd go to this kitchen, do some "witches' brew" and start hallucinating. It was terrible. He thought he was down to his ego-ideal, getting younger and stuff. Sometimes he'd go down to Auerbach's cellar and do ice or something. It was turmoil. You couldn't rely on him. And don't forget, God turned on me, too. That was real bad.

DURAS: How's that?

M. FAUST: He ended up saving this promising animal! Out of sheer vanity. And to piss off Mephistopheles. Benjamin taught me all about how resentful God can get, especially around his lack.

DURAS: I thought Faust got saved because he devoted himself to the earth, announcing a kind of transcendental ecology.

M. FAUST: Are you kidding? He was growing weed, and God

decides to save him, the great technologue wife-beater, diving into the realm of the Mothers!

DURAS: Have another drink.

M. FAUST: I wouldn't get involved with a junkie again. He started out as a doctor, then he started fooling around and conjuring spirits. When we met he was a translator. That kind of moved me, I can't say why. Anyway, he gradually became a phallogojunkie, frying his brains on transcendental striving. At the same time, mind you, getting me pregnant and making my mom OD so we could sleep together without her getting on our case. I think I really like him. But he was an absolute consumer—of knowledge, of desire, you know, a total and deregulated ego scrambling the ethics of dosages. He ran his whole life that way, and left me biting the dust. Which is pretty bad, considering Mephistopheles had predicted it for Faust; he was supposed to *want* to eat dust! I can still remember it in the native language of hell. "Staub soll er fressen/Und mit Lust!" Anyway, *I* was the one who had to bite the dust. That's the only thing I got to consume. Then I turned to God. I've gotta say it felt good. Only twelve steps, and I was off Faust forever. We're talking etenity. But you're never really off the stuff. Anyway, now when I go out, I not only look into the HIV-factor, but they've got to be megasober and into religion, any religion, I don't care which one.

DURAS: Is that so sober? Can't you conceive of something absolutely other than the oppositions you're still hooked into?

M. FAUST: I'm just telling you how I feel. I really got burned, even though I went to heaven, a straight shot. I guess I'm still angry at the whole Faust tradition. It's like going out with a totally creepy rock star who everyone's still cathected onto. I'd like to work out my lingering hostility, and it would help, I guess, if someone would back me up in a different kind of literature.

DURAS: Yeah, well, Goethe had a thing about his couples. Pretty intense at times. I guess I'd do it differently. I'd saturate my couples, watch them dissolve in cafes. Yes, maybe they would know fusional desire but without all that operatic noise. You know what I mean? I like to alcoholize my texts, turn down the volume and let them murmur across endless boundaries and miniscule epiphanies.

(Ernst Jünger has been sitting at a neighboring table; he gets up and approaches the women.)

JÜNGER: May I join you for a moment?

DURAS: Yes, please do. I understand you've been itching for action ever since WWI.

JÜNGER: Well, in a manner of speaking. I couldn't help but overhear your conversation about my old friend, Faust.

M. FAUST: Oh, please! He has too many old friends.

JÜNGER: I don't wish to expose you to telescoping wounds, my dear, but merely to explain the enigma of his persisting reputation—a matter which so clouds your brow. You know, there are those nowadays who regard everything in life as a digital computer. Your man has a lot to do with this ideology—indeed, the strong AI type!

DURAS: Mr. Jünger, you never cease to astonish me with your micrological investigations and global researches. The way you pursue butterflies all over the world is quite enchanting, and I understand you are explaining the virtues of drugs to Martin in an effort to persuade him to join you on a "trip." How fascinating and utterly original an endeavor for a true warrior such as yourself. But I sincerely doubt that you could bring words of comfort to Marguerite.

JÜNGER: That, indeed, would be presumptuous of me. I had only hoped to clarify my appreciation for Faust which is by no means mystifying nor, I hope, insensitive to the harm he has inflicted upon this young lady, not to say this culture. I have tried to construct the conditions for a thanatorium . . .

M. FAUST: Good! Perhaps you should . . .

JÜNGER: My dear lady, I have no intention of increasing your distress, but do try to control your resentment. Of course, I should be happy to leave if that will liberate the space of your interlocution.

DURAS: Don't be absurd, Ernst, we were only trying out some tropes on you. Go on.

JÜNGER: Very well, then. It was to be a thanatorium built upon fractal dimensions of self.

M. FAUST: "Self!" I can barely stomach that word. How much damage has been done in the name of that shell-shocked word!

JÜNGER: Please accept my apologies; some of us older gentlemen have grown quite attached to that word. Perhaps, to accomodate you, I can put it another way. You see, I wanted to test the experience of another limit, a fissure in the law of finality. In short, I wanted to discover a relation to death that might be other than that of skull and crossbones. What you said about the witches' brew intrigued me. You see, I once hitched a ride with my friend, Faust, when he was going to fetch some drug or another.

You must try to understand that Faust not only abused you, but he also abused substances. Nonetheless, there was some cognitive value to his experiments in the domain of drugs. Historically, man has never been older than he has grown now. Excepting perhaps in the so-called Biblical times, of course. Beginning with this era, people often must wait until their forties if they are to inherit from their parents. This will scramble the whole system of inheritance. Indeed, it may reroute what you ladies like to call the patriarchy, not to speak of generational logic.

DURAS: You wanted to tell us about this thanatorium you were designing. I must say, this doesn't seem like a cheerful proposition for social bavardage.

JÜNGER: Ah, but it is terribly social! You see, the witches' brew to which Faust led me was not the narcotica with which the expiring—the dying—are usually let off, stupefied and always already out of it. Don't forget, ladies, we were rather old when we took that trip. The witches' brew offered us a powerful stimulant, opening an altogether other hallucinogenre *in* life, on the edge of being.

DURAS: The mysterious substance did not produce a virile meeting with nothingness, then . . .

M. FAUST: . . . but it created an angle of exteriority in being.

JÜNGER: Precisely!

M. FAUST: As long as you don't forget that I was the excluded negativity that made it possible for you to displace virility.

JÜNGER: I confess that we have a tendency to forget your rather unseemly effacement. But you must know by now that the couple of knowledge is a man-to-man affair. You girls should look into the matter of non-savoir to savor your vertiginous freedom. You, at least, can play with castration. Mind if I smoke?

DURAS: Ernst, we hardly need your advice on savoring our freedom or affirming non-knowledge. These are indulgences of heroic adolescence. But perhaps you can teach us how to die and what you're calling the fractal dimensions of self. Here, have one of mine *(she offers him an elegant looking cigarette, and lights it for him)*.

JÜNGER: I should consider it an honor to do so. But first I must warn you, Marguerite will have to suspend her judgment about drugs. Oh, I quite agree that in some cases they make people unbearably absent, chaotic or, as the Americans charmingly put it, self-serving. You must dispense with your prejudices if you are genuinely to judge my project.

M. FAUST: I understand the contract. I am listening with eagerness.

JÜNGER: While I abhor legalistic jargon, I suppose I should discourse upon the right to drugs as well as upon the supplementary interiority that they produce.

DURAS: Garçon, a bottle of champagne please. *(The music gets louder, the* patronne *puts down her knitting.)*

Installation .03 *In the Thanatorium. Freud advances with Irma.*

FREUD *(helping her with an injection)*: Here, Niemann gave me this. It's the alkaloid obtained from the leaves of the coca bush. One day it will be considered an important substance.

IRMA: So, Niemann finally invented something! Let's call it

cocaine, after your papers. Please make sure that this time the needle is clean.

FREUD: I am very sorry about what happened. Are you still brooding about it?

IRMA: I can't help feeling that it was part of your pact with Fliess, a kind of sacrificial economy. I felt like Marguerite in *Faust*.

FREUD: I'm sure Marguerite would have been happy to have some cocaine if it would get her into a specimen dream, my dear. Actually, I would have liked to analyze her, if only to obtain more information about the trash-body complex, you know, the disposable limit I've been elaborating with you.

IRMA: I sometimes wish you would take up hypnosis again. Schreber and I used to giggle and call it the language-drug. I would like to be put in that trance-like state again, commanded by your words like a neurocomputer, before the labor of analysis. My responsometer was so sensitive then, before you discovered hysteria and trauma. I want to speak a different dialect of the unconscious.

(Faust appears with his groupie disciples. Striving beyond his study, wearing the DataGlove, he offers the guests a witches' brew.)

VOICE OFF: It's not a history of decline but a withdrawal of Being in which we stand. (*Repeat*)

Channel Zero lights up. Split screen. Aztec figures. Witches whose faces change into those of Nietzsche, Poe, Duras, Freud. The Wicked Witch of the West (Emma B.) appears, subsuming all faces: Double, double, toil and trouble, banish realism, conquer nihilism.

JÜNGER: (*Solemnly*) We have passed the zero-line of nihilism. (*He suddenly turns cheerful, evidently pleased with his invention. He gets up to increase the oxygen level*). Even this, my friends, will get you high. I have convoked you here in order to teach the other fold and the conditions of passibility. This thanatorium is yours, or rather, it belongs to that recondite part of you that parallels interiority. My drug manifesto (*he points to a blowup of* Annäherungen) discloses proximities that your philosophies have only dreamt of. They awoke from these dreams in restless exercises of suppression. They thought they were dreaming mama-papa-pipi dreams . . .

FREUD: Now, wait a minute . . .

JÜNGER: . . . and the screen memories of Western culture forgot to think this side of Being, prior to the chivalry of nothingness which . . .

HEIDEGGER: Now wait a minute . . . slow down . . .

JÜNGER: . . . effaces the dionysian ecstasy . . .

NIETZSCHE: I think I'm going under . . .

JÜNGER: I am merely suggesting, dear friends, agents of the heterochronic era, that the originary power of wine itself has been lost to us since the dionysian celebrations. I recall to you those festivals and their uncannily contagious violence.

SAINT THERESA *tunes in:* Spiritual hunger is insatiable. Physical hunger is limited. SPIRITUAL HUNGER IS INSATIABLE.

JÜNGER: Indeed, the question of hunger has not been resolved. Do not forget the intimate rapport that ascetics have to ecstasy.

EMMA B: My father would send us a turkey every year, to commemorate the operation. It was cold on arrival. His leg was transferred symbolically to the turkey. I understood that my papa wanted to be consumed by me. The matter of eating was not resolved in my life, I went to communion, I devoured books. Once, when I was trying to be a good wife, I ate everything in sight. It was my marriage contract.

JÜNGER: I blame America for the word, "intoxication." It has corrupted the history of unprobed intensities and incredible rushes. Their language does not teach the proximity of *Sucht* and *suchen,* craving and searching.

HEIDEGGER: Always the nihilists, these Americans, everywhere the toxic swell. They truly resist the ecstatic. But I must say that, in this regard, I am somewhat American myself. I had to Americanize Nietzsche. It was a good passport for him, allowing his work to spend some time in the detox clinic. This diminished some of those excessive raptures to which he was prone. Still, they have missed the point, on both sides of the line. I will contemplate this line.

JÜNGER *and* HEIDEGGER *murmur, together with the approaching witches:* Rausch, rush, rush. *A windswell*

JÜNGER (*to Heidegger*): I want you to try this, I want to teach you about synthetic drugs, you know, along the lines of our experiments in Freiburg.

HEIDEGGER: Haven't you read what I said in *Being and Time?*

JÜNGER: I had almost forgotten. You were talking about dependency. It's not the same thing. Anyway, that was way before you became fond of poesy and the hallucinations of Trakl. *(They drop acid.)*

HEIDEGGER: This is good, I must concur . . . television without the apparatus.

JÜNGER: Technopowers without technology.

FREUD *advancing with Irma:* This is a lapsus in your thinking, gentlemen, you are now decathecting technology. *(Michaux speaks to Freud about psychomimetic substances and the miraculated subject.)*

HEIDEGGER: It's the only way I can relax.

JÜNGER *(taking a whiff of Michaux's mescaline books)*: You know, I suppose you are right, Sigmund, we are certainly trying to elude the dragnet of calculative time-space tabulations. All we get is statistics. Stats only can show that drugs are dangerous, not the more complicated economies ("is it worth it?") every time you light up a cigarette.

FREUD: Or a cigar.

EMMA: I smoke in order to metabolize my anguish. In the public sphere, it is a provocation. I like to horrify people. They abhor signs of women's narcissism. One smokes for oneself, even against the other. Except sometimes it's intimate to share a cigarette—it punctuates speech and, destining speech's essential silence, it promises your words to forgetfulness.

JÜNGER: My dear young lady, you are beginning to sound like Blanchot.

EMMA: I'm sorry.

HEIDEGGER: I'm sorry, too. Ernst, this stuff you gave me is sheer nonsense. What a paucity of spirit it betokens! I am not interested in the drug deals that went down in the ontic domain as if they were historial. Pushers like Burroughs are still inauthentic. You are miming the picaro, Burroughs, I fear, though you have calculated beyond the algorithm of need.

JÜNGER: For goodness sake, Martin, stop dissing on everyone, just because you made a mistake! What are you thinking?

HEIDEGGER: I am thinking precisely of thinking, I am thinking the higher substance, something that would respond authentically to the call of my ecstatic temporality. I do not want to let go of *Sorge,* by any means. You must find a way, Ernst, of embracing Being-towards-death in your Thanatorium.

JÜNGER: Well, what do you think I've been endeavoring to do, my dear Martin?

HEIDEGGER: Something that would not endanger thinking or reduce it to scholarship or mere experimentation, even as we grow weary. Something that would also shelter us from Emmanuel's extravagant dreams of exteriority. Something that, by virtue of molecular manipulation, would be one step ahead of the law, leaping over legal crackdowns. Something—and why do you suppose we have something rather than nothing, my dear sir?—on the side of thinking. But what is called thinking? What summons or commands it? I would urge the witches to concoct a purée of smart drugs, you know, on the order of choline and other cognitive enhancers. Though this mediation worries me. We have not yet answered the question concerning technology.

JÜNGER: I should hardly consider that high-tech concoction more authentic, though in principle I consider it a rather enticing neuro-adventure. You, on the other hand, are sometimes like a bee—peaceful but with a sting! What you are proposing could mean the end of the genuine rush.

HEIDEGGER: At the end comes the beginning.

(Gustave comes in from the Orient. Baudelaire and Gautier move up to greet him. They light up their pipes.)

JÜNGER: Is nobody hungry?

VOICE OFF: Nobody is hungry . . .
Except for an enraptured prose-being.

WALTER BENJAMIN *(strolling, looking around, stops suddenly):* I was suddenly seized by a ravenous hunger. I was incapable of fearing future solitude, for hashish would always remain.

(Emma Bovary comes forward, puts her hand on Benjamin's arm. Moved, he dissolves in tears.)

CHORUS, *led by* BENJAMIN: That squandering of our own existence that we know in love.

Nano-Installation .04 *Municipal Court. Flaubert, Du Camp, etc., Flaubert's lawyer, Marie-Antoinette-Jules Senard, Member of the Paris Bar, Ex-President of the National Assembly, and former Minister of the Interior, to whom Flaubert will dedicate* Madame Bovary *on April 12, 1857. After a bustle, silence. The judge delivers the verdict. The judge acquits Flaubert and his accomplices with a parting disquisition on taste and a fatherly warning against "a realism which would be the negation of the beautiful and the good."*

Nano-Installation .05 *Six months later. Same place. The court investigates another plant.* Flowers of Evil *is condemned.*

Baudelaire freaks out. His review of Madame Bovary *is postponed, Fl. can't believe it, he wants to help.*

CHORUS: What the fuck?

Nano-Interval .001

EMMA: I'm suffering.

PRIEST: What! *(Taken aback.)* He hasn't prescribed anything for you?

Nano-Installation .06 *After giving birth, Emma keeps on postponing the naming of her child. Finally, she decides upon Berthe. "Since Monsieur was unable to come," writes Flaubert, "Monsieur Homais was asked to be the godfather. All his presents were products from his pharmacy."*

Nano-Interval .002

DELUSIONS OF A NON-ADDICT: "Now he had everything he could wish for. He knew human life from one end to the other, and he looked forward with confidence to what it would offer him in the future."

CHORUS, *in a video of Samuel Beckett's "Le Calmant" (The Downer):* Ah, je vous en foutrai des temps, salauds de votre temps.

(Emma felt the cold of the plaster
descend on her shoulders like a
damp cloth.)

NOTES

1 Charles Baudelaire, *Les Paradis artificiels* (Paris: Gallimard, 1961). Cf. also Théophile Gautier, *La Pipe d'opium, Le Hachich, Le Club des Hachichins* (Paris: Gallimard, 1961).

2 Dominick LaCapra (*"Madame Bovary" on Trial* [Ithaca: Cornell University Press, 1982], p.38), discussing the argument of prosecuting attorney Ernest Pinard, concludes: "The novel is literally poison."

3 Claude Olievenstein, "En Désespoir de Cause," in *L'Esprit des drogues: La Dépendance hors la loi?* ed. Jean-Michel Herviev (Paris: Autrement Revue, 1989), p.30.

4 Letter to Victor Hugo, cited in Francis Steegmuller, *Flaubert and Madame Bovary: A Double Portrait* (Chicago: University of Chicago Press, 1977), p.276.

5 Emmanuel Levinas, *Sur Maurice Blanchot* (Paris: fata morgana, 1975), p.9.

6 Cf. in particular Jean-Luc Nancy, "'Our Probity!': On Truth in the Moral Sense in Nietzsche," trans. Peter Connor, in *Looking After Nietzsche,* ed. Laurence A. Rickels (Albany: State University of New York Press, 1990).

7 Cf. Pierre Deniker, "Intérêt scientifique et dangers sociaux des hallucinogènes (1969)," in *Sigmund Freud et la drogue* (Paris: Editions du Rocher, 1987), p.93.

8 The technologies of drugs and the medias are housed by a supernatural trait. Levinas writes in *Sur Maurice Blanchot,* p.30: "Le discrédit qui frappe le surnaturel dans la pensée et les moeurs de l'Occident n'atteint pas le mystère de l'inspiration."

9 On the side of rigor, Jacques Derrida has offered a more restrained, judicious reading of the rhetoric of drugs in general. See "Rhétorique de la drogue," in *L'Esprit des drogues,* p.209: "Today,

here and now, in my private-public life, and in the fixed situation of 'our' society, I feel rather more inclined toward an ethos, shall we say, that, according to the dominant codes, would be understood as repressive or prohibitory, at least in the case of 'classified' drugs. . . . But to justify the ethos which aligns me with an apparently 'repressive' attitude (in the case of 'classified' drugs) I would not, in the final analysis, rely upon any current discourses or axiomatics."

10 Louis Albrand, "Freud et le panégyrique de la cocaïne," in *Sigmund Freud et la drogue,* p.39.

11 See Pierre Sipriot, "Psychanalyse, drogue: le malentendu," in *Sigmund Freud et la drogue,* p.16.

12 Félix Guattari, "Une Révolution Moléculaire," in *L'Esprit des drogues,* p.18.

13 Jacques Lacan, *Ecrits* (Paris: Seuil, 1966), p.534.

14 William Burroughs, "Letter from a Master Addict to Dangerous Drugs," in *British Journal of Addiction* 53, no.2 1953).

15 *New Jersey* v. *T.L.O.,* 469 U.S. 325 (1985). See also discussion under "Warrantless Arrests and Searches" in Steven Emanuel and Steven Knowles, *Criminal Procedure* (New York: Emanuel Law Outlines, 1988), pp.115ff.

16 Francis Caballero, *Droit de la drogue* (Paris: Dalloz, 1989).

17 William Burroughs, *Naked Lunch* (New York: Grove Press, 1959), p.viii. The book was adjudged obscene in the Superior Court of New York, G.L. c. 272, §§ 28C, 28E, 28F (each inserted by St. 1945, c. 278, §1).

18 Cited in Steegmuller, *Flaubert,* p.283.

19 I refer to Jacques Derrida's usage of "anarchivization" in his contribution to the colloquium "Lacan avec les philosophes," organized by René Major and Philippe Lacoue-Labarthe, Paris, May 1990.

20 Jonathan Culler, "The Uses of *Madame Bovary*" in *Flaubert and Postmodernism,* ed. Naomi Schor and Henry F. Majewski (Lincoln: University of Nebraska Press, 1984), p.4: "Madame Bovary

has been used and will continue to be used to 'construct the intelligibility of our time.'" See also the introduction to the "substantially new translation" of *Madame Bovary* by Paul de Man (New York: W. W. Norton & Co., 1965), and also Harry Levin, "*Madame Bovary:* The Cathedral and the Hospital," in *The Gates of Horn: A Study of Five French Realists* (New York: Oxford University Press, 1963), p.250: "Madame Bovary, c'est nous."

21 Cf. Philippe Lacoue-Labarthe, "History and Mimesis," trans. Eduardo Cadava, in *Looking After Nietzsche.*

22 "Deposition: Testimony concerning a Sickness," in Burroughs, *Naked Lunch,* p.xxxvii.

23 Baudelaire, *Les Paradis artificiels,* 193: "Quels mondes intérieurs! Etait-ce donc là la panacée, le *pharmakon népenthès* pour toutes les douleurs humaines?"

24 Gilles Deleuze, *Différence et répétition* (Paris: Presses Universitaires de France, 1968).

25 Cf. Jacques Derrida, "Plato's Pharmacy," in *Dissemination,* trans. Barbara Johnson (Chicago: University of Chicago Press, 1981).

26 Derrida, "Rhetorique de la drogue," p.207.

27 Paul Virilio, seminar offered at the Collège International de Philosophie, "Télétopies," March 5, 1990.

28 Cf. the Lacano-Derridian analyses in Sylvie Le Poulichet, *Toxicomanies et psychanalyse: Les Narcoses du désir* (Paris: Presses Universitaires de France, 1987).

29 E. Glover, "On the Aetiology of Drug-Addiction," *International Journal of Psychoanalysis* 13 (1932): 298–328.

30 Citations from *Madame Bovary,* ed. Leo Bersani and trans. Lowell Blair (Toronto: Bantam, 1981), p.4. French citations from *Madame Bovary* (Paris: Garnier-Flammarion, 1966). All quotations are from these editions.

31 Hippolyte Lucas, "La Femme adultère," in *Les Français peints par eux-mêmes,* 8 vols. (Paris: L. Curmer, 1840), 3:265.

32 Of course in French *altérer* also means "to be thirsting for." Cf. Jean-Luc Nancy on *différance* and *altération:* "Derrida is a

drunken rabbi," in "Elliptical Sense," *Research and Phenomenology* 18 (1988): 175–90.

33 Lucas, "La Femme adultère," 3:267.

34 Michael Riffaterre, "Flaubert's Presuppositions," in *Flaubert and Postmodernism,* p.183. A fine analysis of adultery until it rocks against this sentence: "Charles does not have what it takes to keep his female satisfied, if only she would give him a chance" (p.183).

35 Ibid.

36 Derrida, "Rhétorique de la drogue," p.202.

37 Ibid.

38 "Ne peut-on dégager de ses antécédents religieux la possibilité, demeurée ouverte, quoi qu'il semble à l'incroyant, de l'expérience mystique? la dégager de l'ascèse du dogma et de l'atmosphère des religions? la dégager en un mot du mysticisme—au point de la lier à la nudité de l'ignorance." Georges Bataille, *L'Expérience interieure,* in *Oeuvres Complètes,* vol.5 (Paris: Gallimard, 1972), p.422.

39 Cf. Flaubert: "My youth drugged me with some kind of opium of boredom for the rest of my life" (letter of October 21, 1851, in Flaubert, *Oeuvres* [Paris: Pléiade edition, Gallimard, 1951]).

40 On Emma Bovary as writer see Naomi Schor, "For a Restricted Thematics: Writing, Speech and Difference in *Madame Bovary,*" trans. Harriet Stone, in *The Future of Difference,* ed. Hester Eisenstein and Alice Jardine (Boston: G. K. Hall, 1980), pp.167–92.

41 I should like to point out that "a blotter" and "*un buvard*" recuperate the link between writing and drinking in the novel, but also refer us to the proper name of its title: buvard, bovary. Cf. "to be blotto," to be smashed, drunk.

42 Cited in Steegmuller, *Flaubert,* p.108.

43 It was Victor Brombert, "Flaubert and the Status of the Subject," in *Flaubert and Postmodernism.*

44 Derrida, "Rhétorique de la drogue," p.205.

45 Steegmuller (*Flaubert,* p.355) publishes a reproduction of the second scenario prepared by Flaubert. The quoted passage was

inserted, in the outline, next to "—departure from Rouen, drunk with love and tears, with the thought of his hair, with champagne—she trembles and perspires in the carriage on the way back as she thinks of it all," and not far from "the thought of seeing him again is intoxicating. . . .—they become lovers again—intoxicating—she tries to return to Charles."

46 The sonic intrusion upon the text has been briefly mentioned by Dennis Porter in "*Madame Bovary* and the Question of Pleasure," in *Flaubert and Postmodernism:* "*Charbovari* is a Joycean neologism that contains an ox and a cart and a discordant noise—"un charivari" (p.121). And: "Above all, perhaps the story of Emma is accompanied throughout by a sonorous subliminal buzz, by a stereophony which is registered by the reader as a reading in the body" (p.135).

47 In Steegmuller, *Flaubert,* p.247.

48 For instance, Théophile Gautier, *La Pipe d'opium,* p.28: "cette mort de quelques heures."

49 Jonathan Culler, "The Uses of *Madame Bovary,*" p.7. Since we are dealing with medical and self-abusive injections, I should perhaps point out that "vaccine" derives from "vache" (cow) and therefore equally belongs to the domain of vealism. In a burst of enthusiasm, Flaubert and his writing partner, Louis Bouillhet began a text which they titled *Jenner; or, The Discovery of Vaccine.*

50 Flaubert's shit fits are legion, his first work being on constipation and the like. The relationship in Flaubert's oeuvre of excrement, intoxication, sexuality, religion, and the trash-body invites further scholarly evaluation. Cf. Flaubert, letter of October 5, 1871, in *Oeuvres:* "We must employ every means to stem the flood of excrement [*merde*] invading us."

51 Sigmund Freud, "Mourning and Melancholia," in *The Standard Edition of the Complete Psychological Works of Sigmund Freud,* ed. and trans. James Strachey (London: Hogarth Press, 1957), 14:249–50. See also the cryptological reading of Flaubert's biography by Eugenio Donato, especially, "Who Signs 'Flau-

bert'?" in *Modern Language Notes* 99 (1984) and "The Crypt of Flaubert," in *Flaubert and Postmodernism.*

52 Laurence A. Rickels, *Aberrations of Mourning: Writing on German Crypts* (Detroit: Wayne State University Press, 1988), p.6. See also Karl Abraham, *Gesammelte Schriften,* ed. Johannes Cremerius (Frankfurt a/M: Fischer, 1982), 2:50.

53 This relationship is commented on in recent theoretically oriented clinical studies. In France, for instance, see Sylvie Le Poulichet, *Toxicomanies et psychanalyse;* Markos Zafiropoulos, *Le Toxicomane n'existe pas* (Paris: Navarin, 1988); François Perrier, *L'Alcool au singulier: L'Eau-de-feu et la libido* (Paris: InterÉditions, 1982) and *Le Corps malade du signifiant* (Paris: InterÉditions, 1984); as well as many others. See also earlier studies, including A. Gross, "The Psychic Effects of Toxic and Toxoid Substances," *International Journal of Psychoanalysis* 14 (1935): 425–38, and R. Savitt, "Extramural Psychoanalytic Treatment of a Case of Narcotic Addiction," *Journal of the American Psychoanalytic Association* 2 (1954): 494–502.

54 See my "Sujet suppositaire: Freud and Rat Man" in *Puns: On the Foundation of Letters,* ed. Jonathan Culler (London: Blackwell, 1988).

55 Flaubert himself had a collection of mummies in his writing and his life. On his desk he displayed two mummy's feet stolen from a tomb. Putting down his lover, Louise Colet, for wanting him too much, he writes: "You occupy a corner of my heart, a sweet place, exclusively your own. . . . Observe yourself carefully: of all the feelings you have ever had, has a single one disappeared? No—every one of them is preserved, is it not? Every one. The mummies in one's heart never fall into dust, and when you peer down the shaft there they are below, looking at you with their open, unmoving eyes" (quoted in Steegmuller, *Flaubert,* 248–49). Shafted or not, Louise continued to feed on Flaubert's letters for her own writing. She sent him back the poem entitled "Fantômes," based on his words.

56 Consider in this regard the necrophiliac adventure in the first version of *La Tentation de saint Antoine,* when Anthony's desire for a young dead girl is expressed: "With a hand slower than that of a mother opening a cradle, you raised the veil and you uncovered her head. . . . you felt her girdle tremble under your fingers and her mouth moved upward towards your lips. You looked at her: on her neck, on the left side, you saw a rose-colored blemish; desire, like a thunderbolt, ran through your vertebrae, you extended your hand a second time" (Flaubert, *La Tentation de saint Antoine: Version de 1849,* in *Oeuvres* 1:379–80). Shoshana Felman offers a subtle reading of mysticism and desire in "Flaubert's Signature: *The Legend of Saint Julian the Hospitable,*" in *Flaubert and Postmodernism.* She understands that "this necessity of crossing, this agonizing passage through the ink stain [which] is, indeed, Julian's predicament" (p.56), sheds light on the nonsurvival kit of Emma Bovary.

57 Harry Levin, *The Gates of Horn,* pp.260–61.

THE UNIVERSITY OF ILLINOIS PRESS
IS A FOUNDING MEMBER OF THE
ASSOCIATION OF AMERICAN
UNIVERSITY PRESSES.

UNIVERSITY OF ILLINOIS PRESS
1325 SOUTH OAK STREET
CHAMPAIGN, ILLINOIS 61820-6903
WWW.PRESS.UILLINOIS.EDU